MAHA-VIRA-CHARITA

MAHA-VIRA-CHARITA.

THE ADVENTURES OF THE GREAT HERO

RAMA.

An Indian Drama in Seven Acts.

TRANSLATED INTO ENGLISH PROSE FROM THE SANSKRIT OF BHAVABHUTI.

BY

JOHN PICKFORD, M.A.

GYAN

Published by

Gyan Publishing House
5, Ansari Road
Daryaganj, New Delhi-110002
Phone: 011-47034999, 9811692060
E-mail: books@gyanbooks.com

Distribution Network
gyanbooks.com
India, USA, Canada, UK, Australia

ISBN: 978-81-212-5971-2 (PB)
First Published, 1871

2nd Impression 2024

Printed at: Gyan Press, Delhi.

MAHA-VIRA-CHARITA
Author: TRANSLATED INTO ENGLISH PROSE FROM THE SANSKRIT OF BHAVABHUTI, JOHN PICKFORD

MAHÁ-VÍRA-CHARITA.

MAHÁ-VÍRA-CHARITA.

THE ADVENTURES OF THE GREAT HERO

RAMA.

An Indian Drama in Seven Acts.

TRANSLATED INTO ENGLISH PROSE FROM THE SANSKRIT OF BHAVABHÚTI.

BY

JOHN PICKFORD, M.A.,

LATE SCHOLAR OF BRASENOSE COLLEGE, AND BODEN SCHOLAR IN THE UNIVERSITY OF OXFORD; PROFESSOR OF SANSKRIT, MADRAS.

LONDON:

TRÜBNER & CO., 60 PATERNOSTER ROW.

1871.

PREFACE.

THE name of Ráma is familiar to all persons acquainted with Hindu literature and worship, and has been famous in Indian story for upwards of three thousand years. His exploits and adventures have ever been a favourite theme with Indian poets and dramatists. They are told at length in the "Rámáyana," an epic poem similar in character to, but more extensive than, the "Iliad" of Homer; and in the "Mahá-Víra-Charita"—which, to a certain extent, is an abstract of the "Rámáyana"—the adventures of Ráma are briefly dramatised.

Modern researches tend to show that the story of Ráma bears with it much in common with the early mythological stories of the Indian, Greek, Roman, Slavonic, and Teutonic nations. In each of these nations it assumed various yet similar forms,—simple and transparent if belonging to an ancient date, but complex and obscure in proportion as they are worked up by more modern hands. Tracing the story to its source, it is purely mythological, and carries us back to a time when the human mind was simple and highly imaginative, and gave to the phenomena of nature an anthropomorphic interpretation. The succession of day and night, light and darkness, was regarded as a battle waged by the bright and dark powers of nature. The change of the seasons was also looked upon as a conflict,—the glorious summer routing the dreary winter, and releasing vast treasures of fruits and grain from the earth where they were imprisoned; while the winter in turn vanquishes the summer, and robs it of its stores. Of this character are many of the hymns of the Rig-Veda, the oldest Sanskrit compositions, wherein we read that*—"Indra (the god of the firmament) slew Ahi (a cloud) and poured out the waters. Thou, Indra, didst strike the first-born of the clouds, then thou didst destroy the delusions of the deluders; then, producing the sun, the sky, and the dawn, thou didst not discover any more a foe."

Such also is the more modern story of the

* Rig-Veda, 1, 32, 1.

Rámáyana. It is not upon the gory battlefields of human strife that its scenes are laid; nor are its heroes mortal men, but the great powers of nature, individualised by the poet, and enlisted into the ranks of toiling mortals, to undergo the same chequered life, and in the same prison-house to be subject to the laws of a perishable existence. The three principal characters are Ráma, Sítá, and Rávana. Ráma is the Solar hero, and the pretended son of the King of Oude, and his frequent title is "descendant of the sun," "born in the race of the sun." Sítá is the wife of Ráma, but has no parentage; the account given of her is, that when King Janaka, her reputed father, was ploughing the ground, Sítá was discovered in the furrow made by the ploughshare; and she is therefore called "sprung from the ground," "not born from the womb." But the meaning of the word itself, which is not once alluded to, indicates her true character; for Sítá really means husbandry, and in this respect corresponds with the Latin Ceres, the patron-goddess of husbandry. Rávana, the king of a country in the South, the capital of which is Lanká, is styled the ruler of night-stalkers:

his authority extends over demons and fiends of darkness, who prowl about intent upon wickedness and marring the good deeds of others. This demon king, in the course of an evil reign, in which he tyrannises over gods and men, at length seizes Sítá and carries her to his capital, Lanká; upon which the Solar hero rouses himself, and going in pursuit, takes Lanká and recovers Sítá, destroying Rávana and his army of demons.

The explanation of this is, either that the powers of night, Rávana and his followers, conquer the bright powers of day, and put an end to the labours of agriculture, until the sun with its increasing rays drives away the darkness, and restores all things as before; or that winter, from the time that the seed is sown in the ground, robs the earth of its splendour until it is displaced by the glowing sun of summer, when the grain springs up once more. The materials from which the epic is constructed consist doubtless of a number of popular sayings handed down from the earliest times, and gradually formed into a connected narrative, which invest with personal attributes the constant changes of day and night, and the rotation of the seasons. This change is expressed in ancient language as a conflict in which the night-fiend with his troops of demons vanquishes the bright powers of day, and carries off to his abode in the west the glorious sunshine, putting an end to the useful works of the husbandman, and leaving him in darkness and dread, until the sun with his increasing rays dispels the gloom and brings back the day to expectant mortals. Thus day by day the struggle goes on, and as the issue of the battle is ever alternating, there comes a period of anxiety and doubt, culminating at length in the still grander conflict of the seasons. Lastly this physical struggle is spiritualised, and takes the form of a combat between good and evil in the world. Ráma is the champion of holiness, Rávana the type of wickedness, and though the evil power is allowed to flourish for a time, yet his reign is short, and goodness in the end triumphs. This, then, is no new story; but one which, under different names, we are well acquainted with. Ever and anon it re-appears throughout the whole period of Sanskrit literature. It is the conflict, so often alluded to in the early Vaidik works, of Indra and Vritra, of the Devas and Asuras. We see clearly its reflection in the story of the Panis, and in that of Vishnu and Bali, and in the myth of Indra and Ahalyá; and it is the same Solar legend that forms the groundwork of the celebrated Indian love-story of Pururavas and Urvacî.

In Greek it is a tale that is told without ceasing, and yet without weariness. We recognise it under the form of Theseus, Persephone, and Hades; Heracles, Alcestis, and Hades; Orpheus and Eurydice; also in the far-famed and later story of Paris and Helen. In Latin it is the story of Hercules and Cacus, Ceres and Pluto. In the Teutonic languages it is told under the names of Odin and Baldr, Beowulf and Grendel. Brief and simple as the story may have been at the outset, each successive age and nation supplied the tradition with fresh characters and scenes, and filled in other details, giving to the legend the appearance of historic truth. In India, these were arranged by the poet Válmíki, and formed into an epic poem, under the title of the "Rámáyana," similar to the "Iliad" of Homer.

There is, however, this remarkable difference in the story as given in the Hindu Mythology, that Ráma combines in his own person qualities that are distributed among several of the Greek and Latin mythological heroes. In his youth, he performs exploits equal in greatness to those of the infant Hercules; and, like Ulysses regaining Penelope, he obtains his bride by drawing a bow that none of the other suitors can bend. As he grew up, he won the esteem of all by his kindness and gentleness of disposition; and, like Baldr in the Scandinavian Edda, or Orpheus, "Whom universal nature did lament," he was loved by the world, and secured the attachment of the beasts of the field and the fowls of the air. But, when Orpheus lost his beloved Eurydice, nature only sympathised with his grief; in the case of Ráma, she did more—she came to his assistance, and rendered him good service in finding and regaining his ravished Sítá. Two vulture kings, Sampáti and Jatáyu, who recall to our mind the winged sons of Oreithyia in the Argonautic expedition, watch over Sítá; and, when she is carried off by the demon king Rávana, Jatáyu throws himself in the path of the ravisher, and endeavours to defeat his wicked purpose; but is slain in the struggle, and with his expiring breath bewails Sítá. Again, as Ráma marches towards the south in search of his bride, the monkeys in great numbers join his standard; and a monkey chief named Hanúman discovers the place where Sítá is concealed. Before, however, the capital of the demons can be reached, a strait of the sea must be crossed; and here the account, differing from the classical myth of the versatile Proteus, assumes a strictly serious tone. The ocean-god is summoned from his abyss of waters to disclose a path across the strait, but refuses to come forth; upon which Ráma discharges an arrow, which penetrates the body of the ocean-god, and compels him with pain and torture to appear and reveal the desired path. The siege of Lanká is then commenced, and as the haughty Laomedon drew a curse upon Ilium, when he oppressed the gods and used harsh threats to Apollo and Poseidon, so the insolent behaviour of Rávana, the demon-king, who had enslaved gods and men, and was ever boasting of his power, had brought on his city Lanká the wrath of the Deities. Its destruction, however, was now fast approaching, and as the battle rages, the gods look on. When Ráma, their favourite, is successful, they rejoice; when the tide of war turns against him, they shudder; nay, they even render him assistance. At length the Solar hero prevails; the night-stalkers are slain, and the demon chief Rávana falls by the hand of Ráma; but even then retains his immortality. Such is the story briefly told, and the limits of this introduction preclude a further discussion of its mythological character.

Thus far, however, an explanation seemed necessary, since attempts are from time to time renewed to melt down such legends, and re-coin from them historic truth; although they bear upon their very face the stamp of mythology, and that, too, not with the figure defaced and the inscription worn out, but palpable and clear, so that all may discern it. True, a few facts may have been drawn into the legend, and possibly the names of a few real persons may be given; but even this is questionable, and, at the best, the supposed facts are so involved in fiction, that it is useless to attempt to separate the real from the unreal.

As the principles of translation here followed are in the main identical with those adopted by most Sanskrit scholars, when clothing the ancient drama of India in a modern dress, it seems unnecessary to say much on that topic. Desirable as it doubtless is to give a translation the best form of which circumstances will allow, still it would be wrong to give up fidelity to the original for a specious affectation of elegance. The sense and character of the author's work must be retained as much as possible, even at the cost of the translator's style. The literature of one modern language may be translated into another with little difficulty, and the turn of expression retained without awkwardness, as it is generally possible to find words and phrases to denote the same conceptions and connote the same attributes. To translate a Greek or Latin author into English is, as every scholar is aware, a far harder task; yet an essentially true rendering may, in most cases, be obtained in good idiomatic English. The chasm is not too great to be bridged over. Oriental, and especially Sanskrit works, will not, however, admit of the same kind of treatment. The difficulty is no longer confined to words and the structure of sentences, but is far more deep-seated, and connected with the whole mode of thought. Hence we often find a single compound word in Sanskrit which cannot be rendered into English except by a long and intricate sentence, with a dependent relative clause for each epithet and allusion. Moreover, the frequent digressions and sudden transitions of Sanskrit compositions, clearly mark them as alien from the thought and language of modern Europe. The canons which are with perfect fairness applied to modern versions of classical authors, are inadmissible with regard to translations from the Sanskrit. For those who wish to form an idea of the drama of India, and for the students of comparative mythology, it is enough if the thought of the writer be accurately reproduced in language that an English reader can clearly understand. The present work will sufficiently fulfil the translator's intention, if it is accepted as faithful and intelligible by those who are qualified to judge. Among the phrases used are some—*e.g.*, the milked ocean—which sound uncouth to an English ear, and would require an apology if now used for the first time. They are such, however, as have been freely admitted in similar translations, and could not be avoided without a tedious periphrasis, and the student will find them fully explained in many familiar works.

The Sanskrit text followed is that published at Calcutta in 1857.

ERRATA.

Page 1, line 22, *for* "Jatáyus," *read* "Jatáyu."
„ 13, „ 8, *for* "Rautathya," *read* "Autathya."
„ 57, „ 14, *for* "Base-born," *read* "a bowman."

MAHÁ-VÍRA-CHARITA:

THE ADVENTURES OF RÁMA.

PERSONS REPRESENTED.

Alaká, the sister of *Lanká*.
Angada, the son of *Váli*.
Arundhatí, the wife of *Vasishtha*.
Ascetic, an attendant of *Vicvámitra*.
Bharata, half-brother of *Ráma*.
Catánanda, the family priest of King *Janaka*.
Catrughna, half-brother of *Ráma*.
Chamberlain.
Charioteer of King *Kucadhvaja*.
Chitraratha, the King of Aerial Spirits.
Companions of *Sítá* and *Úrmilá*.
Cramaná, a sylph rescued by *Ráma*.
Cúrpanakhá, sister of *Rávana*.
Dacaratha, the King of *Ayodhyá*, and father of *Ráma*, &c.
Danu, a fallen demigod restored by *Ráma*.
Handmaid to *Mandodari*.
Hanúmán, a Monkey Chief.
Indra, the God of the Firmament.
Jámadagnya, the son of *Jamadagni*, and enemy of the *Kshatriyas*
Janaka, King of *Videha*, and brother of *Kucadhvaja*.
Jatáyus, a King of Vultures.
Kaikeyí, the mother of *Bharata*.
Kaucalyá, the mother of *Ráma*.
Kinnara, } Aerial spirits.
Kinnari, }
Kucadhvaja, the brother of King *Janaka*, and King of *Sánkásya*.

A

Lakshmana, the half-brother of *Ráma*.

Lanká, the patron goddess of *Lanká*, the capital of *Rávana*.

Málygaván, the Prime Minister of *Rávana*.

Manager.

Mandodarí, the wife of *Rávana*.

Mátali, the charioteer of *Indra*.

Paracuráma, a Bráhman, called also *Jámadagnya*, and the destroyer of the *Kshatriyas*.

Prahasta, the general of *Rávana*.

Ráma, the son of *Dacaratha*.

Rávana, the King of Demons, whose çapital, *Lanká*, was fabled as made of gold.

Sampáti, the King of Vultures.

Sarvamáya, the priest of *Rávana*.

Sítá, the reputed daughter of King *Janaka*.

Sugríva, the brother of *Váli*.

Sumitrá, the mother of *Lakshmana* and *Catrughna*.

Trijatá, a female demon.

Úrmilá, the daughter of King *Janaka*.

Váli, the King of Monkeys, slain by *Ráma*.

Vasishtha, the family priest of King *Dacaratha*.

Vibhíshana, the brother of *Rávana*.

Vicvámitra, the preceptor of *Ráma*.

Yudhájit, the brother of *Kaikeyí*.

MAHÁ-VÍRA-CHARITA;

OR,

THE ADVENTURES OF RÁMA.

Prologue.

BENEDICTION.

SALUTATION to the God, who is self-existent, eternal, who destroys sin, who is without parts * and beyond all rank, the light † of the soul.

(*After the benediction is ended*)—

MANAGER.

To-day, indeed, in the procession in honour of the

* This is an address to Civa, as the one supreme God, who is neither before nor after the others (*tyaktakrama*), and who is without parts (*vibhága*). But *kramavibhága* may be taken as a *tatpurusha* compound, meaning participation in order, *i.e.*, the triple division of the Hindu gods, in which Civa takes the third place in the character of Rudra:—(1.) Brahmá, who creates the world; (2.) Vishnu, who protects it; (3.) Civa, who destroys it.

† Sometimes considered equivalent to *chaitanyam eva jyotish* = "whose glory consists in his knowledge."

divine Civa,* the gentlemen appoint that play to be acted in which there are the exploits of the mighty hero, grand and terrible; in which the language is gentle, and again cruel, and of deep meaning; and in the peerless characters of which the heroic spirit is assigned to each by fine but clear divisions. (*Joyfully.*) Then we must represent the life of the great hero Ráma; thus in truth † they have ordered.

It is the poem of a poet to whom speech is submissive, and that story is of Ráma; and we have obtained an audience that can test the utterance of words, as a touchstone the friction of gold.

I request here to say, that in the south there is a city named Padma-pura; in it dwell certain followers of the black Yajur-veda, descendants of Kacyapa, chiefs ‡ of their school, making holy the company,§ keeping ‖ the five fires, holding vows, drinking the soma, most excellent, repeating the Veda. From their illustrious descendant, who is highly esteemed, and makes the Vájapeya sacrifice, and is a great poet, the fifth in order, the grandson of one whose well-selected name is Bhat-

* This is generally taken to be the appellation of a *Civa-lingam*, *vide* the commencement of *Uttara-ráma-charita*, and *Meghadúta*, ver. 36; but I have seen a commentary on palm-leaves, which explained the compound thus: *Kála*, another name of Civa; *Kála-priyá*=dear to Civa, *i.e.*, Párvatí, his wife; *Kála-priya-nátha*, the husband of Párvatí, *i.e.*, Civa.

† Or, "from their meaning," *i.e.*, no play suits their request so well as the life of *Ráma*.

‡ Or, "teachers of their Veda."

‖ Literally, "purifying the line," *i.e.*, the row of people who sit near them; or, "taking precedence at festivals."—*Wilson*.

§ *See* Manu, chap. iii., ver. 184–186.

tagopála, and the son of the pure in fame Nílakantha, is the poet whose appellation is Bhavabhúti, surnamed Cŕikantha (whose voice is eloquent), and whose mother is Játúkarní, a friend of ours. Thus the gentlemen must understand.

By him, whose teacher is chief of holy ascetics as Angiras is chief of great sages, and who as his name imports is rich in knowledge, was composed this life of the offspring of Raghu, who punishes those who violate justice, whereby the root of sorrow to the three worlds was plucked up, and wherein the great vigour of the heroic spirit abounds, and which is marvellous; through his great love for the hero he composed it.

Therefore you should hallow* it; and that son of a learned sire has said—That holy life of the chief of Raghu's line, which Válmíki,† best of sages and first of poets, traced out, in it the speech of me too, a votary, took pleasure:‡ that life let the good with well-pleased minds revere.

Enter an ACTOR.

The audience is attentive; but, as the composition is new, they desire to learn first the locality of the story.

MANAGER.

That holy descendant of Kucika, Vicvámitra, about to perform sacrifice, after visiting the palace of Dacaratha, born in the line of Ikshváku, a king and saint, whose family priest is Vacishtha, had returned to his own penance-grove; and he, wishing to exalt by charmed

* By listening to it. † Descendant of Prachetas.

‡ *i.e.*, I, as a votary of Ráma, took pleasure in speaking of his exploits.

weapons the victorious and innate valour of Ráma, and seeking to unite that seed of succour to the three worlds with Maithilí,* brought the divine Ráma, who was accompanied by his younger brother and his bow, who is a storehouse of good fortune, praiseworthy for the slaughter of the family of Rávana.

The king of Videha was invited by him; but he, being engaged in sacrifice, sent his brother; and that king, by name Kucadhvaja, now approaches, accompanied by Sítá and Úrmilá.

END OF THE PROLOGUE.

ACT I.

Enter the KING *in a chariot, the* CHARIOTEER, *and the two* PRINCESSES.

KING.

O long-lived ones! Sítá and Úrmilá, to-day you must pay respect to the holy Vicvámitra with faithful mind.

PRINCESSES.

As our young father † orders.

KING.

For he is a fourth holy fire,‡ or a fifth Veda, or a

* Daughter of the king of Mithilá, Sítá.

† *Kanishtha-táta* is equivalent to *pitrivya*, a paternal uncle.

‡ Generally only three fires are mentioned:—(1.) the *gárhapatya*, (2.) *áhavaníya*, (3.) *dakshinágni;* but Vicvámitra is here called a fourth fire as a compliment to his sacred character. In the same way he is called a fifth Veda, though there are only four Vedas.

walking sacred stream, or holiness going about in a body.

CHARIOTEER.

O King of Sánkásya! it is true. Surely no one excels the saint Vicvámitra in greatness; for they who are versed in ancient lore tell of this holy one countless marvels surpassing belief, relating to Tricanku,* Cunacepha,† and the turning of Rambha ‡ into a pillar: therefore you only are a householder praiseworthy among householders in the world, since the management of your family is placed on that saint, whose pacification was implored by the gods headed by Brahmá and by sages, and who is the abode of penance and splendour, who acquired for himself a brahmanical state,§ and who is the dwelling-place of knowledge.

KING.

Good, good! for you speak, O Charioteer, what is both pleasant and true. Surely these holy and great saints, to whom the supreme spirit has been revealed, indicate by their visit great prosperity.||

Darkness fades, calmness increases more and more; even after once conversing, happiness spreads both in this and the next world; then a close union gives a greatness beyond expression; the words of the calm bear immeasurable fruit.

* *Vide Rámáyana, bála-kánda*, 57 60.

† *Ibid.* 61-62. ‡ *Ibid.* 64.

§ Vicvámitra was by birth a Kshatriya, but became a Bráhman by his penance.

|| Literally, "have their meetings resulting in great prosperity."

CHARIOTEER.

The home of that saint, called the ground of the famous hermitage, is in view, pleasant with neighbouring forests which are green, and surrounded by the river Kaucikí. Why need I say more? The son of Kucika with two others is coming here to meet you.

KING.

If so, we will descend from the chariot. (*After alighting with the Princesses.*) O Charioteer! Charioteer! let the troops be warned that the grounds near the hermitage are not to be trodden by any one.

CHARIOTEER.

As you command. [*Exit.*

Enter VICVÁMITRA, RÁMA, *and* LAKSHMANA.

VICVÁMITRA (*to himself*).

Prosperous acts which cause the death of demons must be done by the skilful on this good day; and the marriage of Ráma with Vaidehí,* and our entrance into the sacrificial state, must be made; and the many marvellous actions of Vishnu, wearing the form of Ráma, must be determined for the welfare of the world: then indeed we may wholly rejoice. And thinking it our duty, we sent word to the king and sage who rules Mithilá, "You, although engaged in sacrifice, are invited to our sacrifice; but let Kucadvaja with Sítá

* Another reading is *Raghúdvahasya cha kule* = "the marriage of Vaidehí and Ráma must be made, and in our family preparation for sacrifice must be made."

and Úrmilá be sent;" and that has been done by our dear friend.

PRINCES.

O sire! who then is this noble man whom you, holy as you are, go forth to meet?

VICVÁMITRA.

Kingly saints born in the race of Nimi are surely well known in Videha. Their descendant is now the aged King Síradhvaja, to whom the saint Yájńavalkya chanted the whole of the Veda.*

PRINCES.

In whose house is revered that bow of Civa.

VICVÁMITRA.

Yes.

PRINCES (*with surprise*).

Then, indeed, there is another marvel also there—a virgin not born from the womb.

VICVÁMITRA (*smiling*).

That also is true. But he, being engaged in sacrifice, out of affection for me sent his younger brother Kucadhvaja here to my house as I was about to sacrifice; therefore you, my sons, ought to show courtesy to this learned king.

PRINCES.

True.

* The *Cukla-yajur-veda*, or *Vájasaneya-cákhá*, of which *Yájńavalkya* is the reputed author—*pára* + *ayanam* : *sámagryena adhyayanam.*

KUCADHVAJA (*looking intently at them*).

Who are these two, holy and handsome by nature? But this much I know, surely they are sons of a kingly man, and their Vaidik * rite is performed? Oh! pleasing are the forms of these two of the second caste and the first order of life, and whose age is young: for at their back are two quivers, the arrows of which are kissed by their locks of hair; and on their chest, which has the purifying mark of collected ashes,† is a deer-skin; and their under-garment, tinged with red dye,‡ is held up by a girdle of the múrví plant; § and in their hand is a bow, and a bracelet strung with nuts,|| and a staff of the fig-tree.

PRINCESSES.

Truly they are of pleasing aspect.

KING (*going near*).

Sire! I greet thee.

VICVÁMITRA.

Oh! I look on thee as my own child, who art in good health; and art come hither from the palace of the holy king; therefore, embrace. (*After embracing.*) Is the King of Videha, who is engaged in sacrifice, happy? and the descendant of Gotama Catánanda, the family priest of the Janakas?

* *Apastamba dharma-sútra*, i. 1, 2.

† Another reading is *stoka*, a small mark of ashes.

‡ *Mánjishtham rájanyasya—Apastamba dharma-sútra*, i. 1, iii. 1.

§ *Manu*, ii. 42.

|| Another reading is *dando' pare*, in the other hand a staff.

KING.

Truly the noble king is well, with his family priest, the descendant of the saint of great penance, when you attend to the rites of his family.

PRINCESSES.

We make obeisance.

KING.

Here is Sítá, who came forth from the place of sacrifice furrowed by the plough; and this second is Úrmilá, the very daughter of Janaka.

VICVÁMITRA.

May good fortune attend.

LAKSHMANA (*aside*).

A marvel is this noble lady of wondrous birth.

RÁMA.

Her birth is from the altar of the gods; her sire is a king who repeats the Veda; her form, pleasing and bright, excites my love.

KING.

O sire! who are these two religious students of royal family that follow you, like majesty and valour led by holiness?

VICVÁMITRA.

Ráma and Lakshmana, sons of Dacaratha.

PRINCES (*approaching with modesty*).

O sire! we greet you.

KING.

By good fortune I behold the sons of the great King Dacaratha. (*After embracing.*) Nowhere, save in the race of Raghu, would the birth of these princes be proper. Whence, save from the milked ocean is the origin of the moon and the jewel of Vishnu? For this story, like nectar to the ear, we heard aforetime; that sons, pious and pleasing, were obtained by the King of Kocala with difficulty, through the holy rites of Rishya-cringa; and these sons, four in number, seeking the completion of glorious action, lead a bachelor life. Therefore, we pray * for an increase of happiness from blessings pronounced by you: but the excellence of the family of Raghu is indeed well known. Whom the holy descendant of Mitra and Varuna instructs in the rite of sacrifice made pure by sacred texts, and with whom ever rests the duty, not shared by others, of protecting subjects,—the greatness of such kings, born in the exalted line of Manu, son of the sun, comes not indeed within the range of our speech or mind.

VICVÁMITRA.

You only, who are untiring in holy acts, and whose fame is great and purifying, and who know their great happiness, are fit to praise them. Friend! the people are entering the houses to repose; therefore, we will sit for a moment in the shade of this Vikankata-tree.

[*All walk round and sit down.*

* The meaning, I think, is, "We pray for an increase of happiness, though there is really no need; for the family of Raghu is great already."

(*A voice is heard behind the scenes.*)

Success! success to Rámachandra, the ruler of the worlds! Success!

[*All look with surprise.*

KING.

Sire! who is this holy lady?

VICVÁMITRA.

'Tis the true wife of the great saint Gotama Rautathya, and her name is Ahalyá, of whom Catánanda, descendant of Angiras, was born: her Indra loved, therefore they call him, who assailed the wife of Gotama, by name, "Ahalyá's paramour." Then the sage was wroth; upon her, his married wife, he invoked blindness: she to-day, by the glory of Rámabhadra, is released from that sin.

KING.

How is it that this boy, born in the race of the sun, has such matchless power natural to him, and beyond limit?

SÍTÁ (*beholding him with love and affection, and turning aside*).

Truly his disposition corresponds to the structure of his frame.

KING (*sighing*).

Sítá would indeed have been given to Ráma, who is like her, and whose glory is pure, and who is a moon in line of Dacaratha, had not the noble Janaka made the marriage-terms unalterable,—consisting in stringing the bow of Civa.

Enter an ASCETIC.

ASCETIC.

The priest of Rávana, an aged Rákshasa, named Sarvamáya (all-deceit), desires to see you on the king's business.

PRINCESSES.

Oh! a Rákshasa.

PRINCES.

He is an object of great curiosity.

KING *and* VICVÁMITRA (*after reflecting*).

Oh! let him come. [*Exit* ASCETIC.

Enter the RÁKSHASA.

RÁKSHASA.

Rávana (the ten-faced one), being forbidden by Mályaván, his grandfather, to carry away Sítá, sent me to Mithilá, the capital, to choose the king's daughter, who is not born from a womb: and that king, as he was there sacrificing, was seen; and at his command I am come to see Kucadhvaja and the descendant of Kucika. [*Thus speaking, he walks round.*

RÁMA *and* LAKSHMANA (*towards* SÍTÁ *and* ÚRMILÁ *respectively, and speaking to themselves*).

How is it that this lady pleases my eye like collyrium of nectar?

SÍTÁ *and* ÚRMILÁ (*in the same manner towards* RÁMA *and* LAKSHMANA).

How is it that my gaze is fixed on this delight of my eye?

RÁKSHASA (*approaching and looking*).

This is Sítá of wondrous form; she is fit to be the wife of my lord. O saint! salutation to thee. I trust the king is well.

BOTH.

Welcome. Sit here. Is that king of yours well, whose mandate Indra reveres with his head from which the diadem is falling?*

RÁKSHASA (*approaching*).

My lord is well, and the great king has sent word to you thus, "That jewel of virgins, not born from a womb, is yours; and we are suppliants. If there is a jewel anywhere, it comes down to us even from Indra. The dependency of the maiden is well known; and through her surrender I will become your kinsman, and Pulastya, Pulaha, and Prashtha will be your relations.

SÍTÁ.

Alas! alas! the Rákshasa asks for me.

ÚRMILÁ.

How so?

(*The* KING *and* VICVÁMITRA *consider.*)

LAKSHMANA (*aside*).

Sir, sir! dost thou not see that the king of demons asks for this goddess?

* *i.e.*, To whom Indra, though a god, bows so low that his crown falls off.

RÁMA.

Dear brother! another too without fear may claim the maiden, because of her unmarried state; how much more, then, may the conqueror of the worlds, the great grandson of the Supreme?

LAKSHMANA.

From thy excessively good nature, respect is shown even to this demon, thy natural enemy, who by the destruction of the three Vedas robs us of our glory as warriors, and who slew the king and saint Anaranya, descendant of Ikshváku.

RÁMA.

He is an enemy; therefore, perhaps, he may be slain; but thou shouldst not revile as a common person him whose penance is beyond limit, and who is a great hero and no common mortal.

LAKSHMANA.

What heroism has he who has violated the law of heroes?

RÁMA.

Say not so. Because, though wise and born in a noble race, he swerved from the rightful path, what shall we say of this? It is another matter; * all virtues dwell not together. Save the divine son of Jamadagni, by whom the six-headed one was easily conquered, who is such a warrior as he,— seeing that he obtained victory over the world without hindrance?

* It affects not his valour.

RÁKSHASA.

Oh! what are you thinking about here?

Let the daughter of the earth, like the goddess of warriors, recline on the breast of that husband who is the conqueror of the world,—that breast which shines with scars of wounds fixed and implanted* by splinters of the thunderbolt, which was shivered at once by the contact; and upon which the might of the tusks of the elephant of Indra was exerted in vain, for they were broken; and on which the circle of the garland was hung by the goddesses of Nandana.

[*A noise behind the scenes.*

KING.

O sire! the great sages who have been invited to the sacrifice are assembling with their wives and sons from all quarters, and by them the noise blended with the cry of voices is made.

[*All rise up.*

LAKSHMANA.

Who is this, that, making the sky to re-echo with the sound of large ornaments moving to and fro, and consisting of bracelets harshly tinkling, and rib bones, and large skulls which are filled with entrails, and possessing a body terrible by the weight of breasts, that swing to the side and move upwards, horrid by reason of the mass dense with filth and blood which is first drunk and afterwards vomited up, runs along inflated with pride?

* *Pratyupta*, sown over, spread over.

VICVÁMITRA.

She is the daughter of Suketu, and wife of Sundágura, the mother of Márícha, a terrible fiend named Tátaká.

PRINCESSES.

O sire, sire! that evil woman is terrible.

KING.

Fear not, long-lived ones.

VICVÁMITRA (*touching* RÁMA *on the chin*).

Son, let her be slain.

SÍTÁ.

Alas! alas! He, and no other is appointed to this.

RÁMA.

Sire, she is only a woman.

ÚRMILÁ.

Heardst thou that, sister?

SÍTÁ (*with surprise and affection*).

The nature of his mind is unlike others.

KING.

Good! Truly Rámabhadra is a descendant of Ikshváku.

RÁKSHASA.

Here is the famed Ráma, son of Dacaratha, who is fearless even in the face of danger arising from the fierce Tátaká; and, being appointed to destroy her, hopes to succeed by reason of her womanhood.

VICVÁMITRA.

Let the boy hasten; dost thou not see the large collection of Bráhman people in front?

RÁMA.

Thus your majesty determines.

Your judgment, which has attained an equality with the Veda, because of its freedom from all vice, is the standard of good and evil.

[*Thus speaking he walks round and leaves the stage.*

SÍTÁ.

Alas! he is gone indeed. Alas! alas! like a rush of destructive wind the wicked woman assails the high-souled one.

KING (*twanging his bow*).

Ah, wicked woman! stop, stop.

ÚRMILÁ.

See, now my father too has set forth.

LAKSHMANA (*smiling*).

Your majesty should watch * Tátaká.

She is already dead, with a shower of blood eddying and foaming and streaming equally from the two cavities of her huge nostrils,† displaying the contraction of her quivering limbs, caused at once by the speed of the excellent arrow, which falls and pierces the vitals of her heart.

* There is no need to do aught but merely to look on.

† *Kutíra*, literally a hut it is here used, I think, to indicate her huge, open nostrils.

PRINCESSES.

A marvel! a marvel! 'Tis pleasing to us.

KING.

Oh, the brave fighting of the king's son!

RÁKSHASA.

Alas! noble Tátaká, what does this mean? Gourds sink in the water, and stones float. Surely this day the majesty of the king of demons was shaken. A fresh insult came from a mere stripling; and, as I stood here, I beheld the death of my kinswoman. Sorrow and old age impede me. How shall I act?

VICVÁMITRA.

This is but the prelude.

RÁKSHASA.

Oh there! What is your answer to us?

VICVÁMITRA.

In this matter Síradvaja decides, for Kucadhvaja is the youngest; since he is the father of that maiden, the chief of the race, and our king.

RÁKSHASA.

He also says that Kucadhvaja and Vicvámitra decide.

VICVÁMITRA (*to himself*).

This is the season for the gift of good fortune, namely, the divine weapons, and the fortunate moment is now. (*In a loud voice.*) Friend Kucadhvaja! the seeds of true knowledge of the full use of spells for divine weapons, with all their secrets, namely, their awaking, shooting, and recalling, obtained by me from Kricácva, by vows and services to my teacher, are now through his favour made manifest to Rámabhadra, with their words and meaning. Ancient saints, headed by Brahmá, after doing penance for more than thousands of years for the good of the Supreme, saw these weapons wrought by penance like their own glories.

KING.

The race of Raghu is favoured.

LAKSHMANA.

By good fortune there is the sound of the drums of the gods, and a shower of flowers.

RÁKSHASA.

Ah! even the gods are pleased with the act that is adverse to my king.

LAKSHMANA.

How is it that suddenly all the quarters of heaven seem tinged with gold melted and heated; and, from the yellow hue, the day shines as though it were overcast with the twilight; and by reason of the multitude of divine weapons, the sky seems filled with flaming comets, and yellow with lightnings which are flashing in every part? The ray of the sun gives up its power, rapidly acquired and then in turn lost, through the splendour of these weapons, flaming everywhere, in each quarter, with a glitter surpassing the sun's light.

PRINCESSES.

By reason of the flash of light yellow with the mass of lightning, which flames on all sides, eyes seem to issue forth.

RÁKSHASA.

Oh! the glory of the divine weapons cannot be approached; which, as it spreads around, reminds me of the combat fought by the city-destroyer (Indra) and Rávana. The thunderbolt shot by Indra as he bent forward with his whole strength, and which, after striking the chest of Rávana, had a huge piece broken off by the friction, with just such speed filled the sky with thousands of lightnings as did my lord's loud and angry laughs, red with the flames in his mouth.

VICVÁMITRA.

O Rámabhadra! make obeisance, and then leave the divine weapons. Of these which surpass Brahmá, Indra, Kuvera, Rudra, Varuna, Práchínavarhi, the Maruts, and the fire of destruction, and which are divine, and consist of spells from the Veda, and which are excellent by reason of their matchless splendours, like those of penance,—the power of each one is able to preserve or destroy the three worlds.

(*A voice is heard behind the scenes.*)

I am a suppliant here, and this is our request: Let this gift of the divine weapons be shared by Lakshmana.

VICVÁMITRA.

Rámabhadra, be it so.

LAKSHMANA.

Oh, the favour! I think my mind possesses expanded wisdom, and is powerful beyond thought, and is made of splendour, through the revealing of this knowledge.

(*A cry behind the scenes.*)

Ráma, Ráma of the strong arm! we depend on thee. Do thou with thy brother protect us, with the sanction of Vicvámitra.

PRINCESSES.

The gods speak! Oh, the marvel!

(*A cry behind the scenes.*)

O ye collections of divine weapons, this day Ráma having obtained you from Vicvámitra the friend of the world by good acts, is victorious. Do you come whenever you are thought of. Go now to your place. Salutation to you!

LAKSHMANA.

The arms have vanished at the word of the noble one.

KING.

The panegyrist, who has made an attempt to praise the good fortune, great and without limit, of thee, whose devotion is brilliant, and splendour vast, and majesty immeasurable in the world, not finding either in word or thought power of sufficient range, despairs, with his utterance impeded,* and feels disgust with himself.

* I have some doubt about this, for the compound may be translated "having trembling produced," *i.e.*, being filled with fear; still, the general meaning of *pratihata* is obstructed, impeded.

I envy King Dacaratha, who is adorned by Rámabhadra, favoured by you; but we have been deceived by you, since we are not united with such a son-in-law.

VICVÁMITRA.

Why, even on this day, is there this misconception about us?

KING.

'Tis past.

VICVÁMITRA.

Then let that bow become visible before Rámabhadra, which gives you its presence merely by meditation, through the favour of Civa.

KING.

Be it so.

[*He meditates, and bows his head.*

RÁKSHASA (*to himself*).

Some other matter is begun by them. (*Aloud.*) O Kucadhvaja! how long do you consider?

KING.

I have already said—"The king decides."

RÁKSHASA.

And I have answered, that he too says—"Kucadhvaja decides."

KING.

Even so.

(*Behind the scenes, after a confused noise, a voice is heard.*)

The bow, which seems as if made of a thousand

gleaming thunderbolts, and which makes an end of demons, and which is kindled with the splendours of the gods, becomes visible before Ráma.

SÍTÁ (*aside*).

Now I am filled with doubt.

VICVÁMITRA (*speaking to the King*).

And the boy fixed his staff-like arm on the bow, as an elephant plants its trunk on a mountain.

ÚRMILÁ.

May it be so.

KING.

And it was drawn, so that the string twanged.

ÚRMILÁ (*embracing* SÍTÁ, *who is delighted and ashamed.*)

By the favour of heaven we prosper.

KING (*with surprise*).

And it is broken!

RÁKSHASA (*speaking to himself*).

Alas! the power of Rámabhadra, vile as he is, is assailing everything.

LAKSHMANA.

The twanging sound, that rose from breaking the huge bow of Civa, which was bent easily by his arms and was like a drum to foretell the actions of the noble youth, and the harshness of which is concentrated and whirling within the hollows of the universe, blending with the cavities of the sky, which is suddenly overspread,—how is it that it does not cease even now?

KING (*with joy and delight*).

Come, come! O descendant of Raghu, Rámachandra! I kiss thy head! At length I embrace thee. Clasping thee to my heart, I will bear thee day and night, or I will salute thy two lotus-like feet.

RÁMA (*entering*).

What! through excess of affection is there then a violation of rule?*

VIÇVÁMITRA.

Your majesty is the superior, and the child-like Rámabhadra is your pupil.

KING (*bowing to him*).

Sire, those your blessings to Sítá are fulfilled by her possessing Ráma. At this very festival Úrmilá shall be given by me to Lakshmana.

PRINCESSES (*with tears*).

Alas! we are given in marriage.

RÁKSHASA (*speaking to himself*).

That which was to be seen, has been seen.

VIÇVÁMITRA.

'Tis well, we bow in assent; but you must hear the rest.

* In an elder making obeisance to a young man.

KING.

Give me your commands.

VICVÁMITRA.

Thy two daughters, Mándaví and Crutakírti, I request for Bharata and Catrughna.

RÁKSHASA (*to himself*).

See the family respect paid towards a warrior by a Bráhman who dwells in a forest.

KING.

Sire, why should we hesitate at all about this? But, I am dependent on the will of another in this matter.

VICVÁMITRA.

On whom?

KING.

On your honour, for one.

VICVÁMITRA.

On whom besides?

KING.

On the noble Síradhvaja and Catánanda, descendant of Gotama.

VICVÁMITRA (*smiling*).

I will speak in behalf of Síradhvaja and Catánanda.

KING.

Your honour now decides. To whom is not the union of the Janakas and the Raghus agreeable, in which you who are a source of happiness, are both the giver and receiver?

VICVÁMITRA.

Boy Cunacepha, go to Ayodhyá, and tell the holy Vasishtha at our command: "Those four daughters of the king in the race of Nimi were given and received by me alone, acting in behalf of Vasishtha and Gautama, for the four sons of Raghu; therefore, after inviting all the great sages, and following the great king, Dacaratha, come to the city of Vaideha. Then, at the end of the sacrifice, performed by me and the king of Mithilá, the princes, whose good fortune is enhanced by the rite of tonsure, shall marry."

PRINCES (*speaking to themselves*).

This is more and more pleasing.

PRINCESSES.

Oh! a separation of us sisters will not now take place.

RÁKSHASA.

Oh there! even to-day listen to a word of duty. It is indeed in vain that this maiden is given to another. Paulastya asks with courtesy. Even when there is such a praiseworthy union as this, you show no respect, and you have no desire for friendship with the lord of the three worlds: but assuredly Sítá shall in another way go to our Lanká. Therefore, let there not be here the law that is used against the captive women of the city of Indra.

[*Behind the scenes a confused noise.*

KING.

Who then are those two, that, terrible as thunder-clouds out of season, rush by with a crowd?

VICVÁMITRA.

They are Subáhu and Márícha, sons of Sunda and Upasunda, followers of Rávana, terrible, causing hindrance to sacrifices; therefore boys, Ráma and Lakshmana, let this hindrance to sacrifice be destroyed.

PRINCES.

As you command.

[*Thus speaking they walk proudly round.*

PRINCESSES.

In this case now how will it be?

RÁKSHASA.

Ah! that which is done seems well, but the course of things may be reversed; therefore, when I have seen the end of the matter, I will report it to Mályaván.

KING (*twanging his bow*).

Child Rámabhadra, child Lakshmana, calmly vanquish this wild foe. I am come to your side.

VICVÁMITRA (*smiling and taking him by the hand*).

O king, come here! see the matchless valour of Ráma with his younger brother: for, like the fierce rites of the Atharva-Veda, he destroys all the enemies of the Supreme.

[*Exeunt omnes.*

END OF THE FIRST ACT.

ACT II.

Enter MÁLYAVÁN.

MÁLYAVÁN (*seated and thoughtful*).

Oh, from the day that I heard the story about the famous hermitage* from Sarvamáya, ever since then the king's son, who repelled afar off like a blade of grass the son of Tátaká, though huge as a mountain, the slayer of Subáhu too, and the foe of Tátaká, pains me to the heart. And the slaughter of their many followers in a moment by one man,—how this can be, is the cause of my wonder.

That bow which the lotus-born one made by the great powers of the nectar-eating gods, that bow of Civa, Ráma broke in sunder,—the hero who of matchless power obtained from the saint Vicvámitra, pupil of Kricácva, instruction in divine weapons which produces victory. To him the wondrous gift of arms hostile to Rávana was forcibly made in good season by the haughty saint, while our ambassador looked on. For the outrage of seizing Sítá as a captive was forbidden that king, and the sovereignty over the gods is in our case brought to a feeble state, since an auspicious act, beginning with the sound of the blessing, was then performed by them. Everything generally suffers a change when majesty is weakened.

What! is the child Cúrpanakhá come?

* The abode of Vicvámitra.

Enter CÚRPANAKHÁ.

CÚRPANAKHÁ.

Success, success to my grandfather!

MÁLYAVÁN.

Child, sit down. What news is there with the king?

CÚRPANAKHÁ.

'Tis said the marriage has taken place, and the excellent bow of Civa, which brings victory, has been sent to Ráma by the great sage Agastya.

MÁLYAVÁN.

Those weapons, the power of which in the worlds is beyond conception, come to Ráma from the divine sages. (*Thoughtfully*). A weapon that fails not and the favour of Bráhmans belong to a Kshatriya; and that glory of a Kshatriya, when united with divine knowledge, is difficult of approach.

CÚRPANAKHÁ.

Why such thought as this about a mere man?

MÁLYAVÁN.

Child, not so indeed. For the descendant of Raghu by his birth alone has somehow such a form in the world. This is strange. But what has he to do with a mortal state, when his actions are sung by gods and demons? Saints and gods grant him in all things power beyond thought; and it was from a mortal only that the Supreme warned us of danger, at the time that he granted the boon. Besides, he is by nature the champion of holiness. We violate holiness: a natural enmity * with a powerful rival has arisen to us.

ÇÚRPANAKHÁ.

What doubt? While the ten-headed Rávana remains thus, with head bent, and his rolling eyes robbed of their twenty glances well-nigh closed, so long, I know, the speed of the painful workings of his heart, which is terrible, will not cease thus.

MÁLYAVÁN.

Ah! indeed. How is it that we and the seven sages deserving of worship, creators of worlds, teachers at the beginning of ages, sons of the Supreme, were not welcome relations to the king of Videha? But let that be. How is it that feebleness has arisen in the heart of Paulastya, lord of the world, who is bright by reason of his penance, hard to approach, and of bright glory? Again, when his suppliant state was made known, the gaining of the prize accrued not to my lord; but, on the contrary, Dáçarathi, who is working mischief, and whose actions are hostile, is united to that maiden. How is it that the haughty ten-faced hero, the lord of the worlds, bears the rise of an enemy, and the decline of his own respect and fame, and (the loss of) the pearl of maidens?

CHAMBERLAIN (*half entering from behind the scenes*).

The messenger whom you despatched to Paraçu-ráma

* An enmity which we sought not, but which was likely to follow, and might be inferred from our respective actions.

has brought this palm-leaf, on which letters are written with the juice of the Tamála.

[*He lays it down and departs.*

(MÁLYAVÁN *takes it and reads.*)

Greeting! Paracu-ráma from the island Mahendra salutes Mályaván the minister at Lanká.

CÚRPANAKHÁ.

How like a chief he writes in noble style!

MÁLYAVÁN.

Here indeed, saluting the king of Lanká, the follower of the great Mahecvara, he says, "This you know, that I have given promise to protect the saints who dwell near the sacred streams of the Dandaká forest; and it is reported that certain people, Virádha, and the headless Danu, and others, are there trespassing: therefore you should forbid them, and thus adopt a good course of life, which will be gratifying to us and will please Mahecvara. If you refrain from trespass against Bráhmans, it will tend to your welfare, and the son of Jamadagni will be your friend; if not, he will be angry."

CÚRPANAKHÁ.

This speech displays self-confidence combined with gentleness, and is deep and haughty.

MÁLYAVÁN.

Oh! what can we say? Truly he is the son of Jamadagni. That saint,—whose tranquillity is increased by his excellences of birth, penance, learning, valour, and actions; and who, after renouncing all things, abides in a state free from all desires,—through his friendship for the followers of Civa instructs us reluctantly and from no wish of his own; but, like a chieftain, in his every act he becomes merciless indeed.

[*Thus he reflects.*

CÚRPANAKHÁ.

What are you reflecting upon?

MÁLYAVÁN.

Child! if the breaking of the bow becomes known to the pupil of Civa, he will not endure it: then should the death of both ensue in the battle by reason of their rage, this will be most pleasing to us. But even in the victory of either, should the hero who causes the death of Kshatriyas conquer the king's son, the angry one will not cease without slaying him; and thus will be effected our wish, namely, the death of Ráma. But should the descendant of Ikshváku conquer; he will not, since he is a friend to Bráhmans, slay the holy sage. He will employ the weapon, even though laid aside, against him * who is endowed with prosperity, and this will be worst of all.

CÚRPANAKHÁ.

What difference will there be?

MÁLYAVÁN.

If the son of Jamadagni, who wears a different vow,

* Rávaṅa.

should slay the descendant of Raghu, still even after killing him he will be just the same; but let this view be taken,—should the king's son, who strives to excel, kill by reason of his great power and energy that saint who is most happy, and who conquers by his holiness, all will acknowledge him when he is victorious. Then, indeed, all the gods, whose anger is increased by his (Rávana's) violent attacks, will forcibly appoint him as their chieftain; for a natural enmity* ever arises towards the victorious demons, because they are disdainful. Ráma, whose actions are holy and pleasing even though he has the power by which evil deeds may be wrought, will be lord of the universe; he who inflicts proper punishment on that saint, who made a happy commencement of the rite of finishing † the story of all the Kshatriyas, in the person of Kárttavírya, whose deeds were violent by reason of his defeat of Paulastya.

CÚRPANAKHÁ.

Therefore what think you now about this matter?

MÁLYAVÁN.

We must excite Paracu-ráma.

CÚRPANAKHÁ.

In the other case it will be a grievous sin.‡

* Or, "the enmity of their subjects," *i.e.*, of those whom the demons have enslaved.

† Of exterminating them to a man.

‡ If Ráma kill Paracu-ráma, Málvaván will incur the guilt of causing a Bráhman's death.

MÁLYAVÁN.

Against that also, to the best of our power, we will employ a remedy. But if the elements are the same, if his powers are the same as aforetime, then we cannot expect the defeat of Paracu-ráma. Therefore arise, we will go to Mahendra to incite Jámadagnya to start for Mithilá; and the holy descendant of Bhrigu must there be seen. He, who is haughty from his noble nature, and of the greatest purity, and beyond all in goodness, calm, and giving pleasure to all, like a mine of holiness, when seen will increase our goodness, and will dispel sin through the excellence of his sovereign state and the ripe purity of his penance.

[*They rise up, and walk round, and leave the stage.*

(*Behind the scenes a voice is heard.*)

Ho there! let the noble chamberlains belonging to the city of Videha tell Rámabhadra, who is gone to the chamber of the princess, that "the hero, through whose anger Kárttavírya of old had the stock of his family rendered like to a tree shorn of its stalwart branches, for he was reft of his huge arms, and had the joints of his massive shoulders cleft by the axe, hard as he was to vanquish, and though he had humbled easily, as in play, the pride in battle even of Paulastya, whose arms were made famous by acquiring victory over the three worlds through his strength which heaved up the mountain Kailása,—that hero, the son of Jamadagni, by whom the exercise of the art of warriors was performed without defect thrice seven times, and who by cleaving the Krauncha pass opened for the swans a descent, that before was not, to the land;—he, the conqueror of the enemy of Táraka,* who is followed by hosts of divine warriors headed by Heramba and Bhringa, is come asking for you through anger at the breaking of the bow of Civa his teacher."

Enter RÁMA, SÍTÁ, *and her* FRIENDS.

RÁMA (*with firmness and haste*).

Oh! the lord of the race of Bhrigu, who is a great mine of good fortune, the pupil of the revered god who destroyed the cities of demons, and whose every act is pure by his sacred learning, who is even desirous of seeing me, must be seen by the shame-faced bride, and she must cast aside her modesty. Natural friendship, concealed by his high birth, is made manifest to me from this threatening.

SÍTÁ.

Oh, my friends! how will this end?

FRIENDS.

Prince, away with such haste!

RÁMA.

Valour knows not a want of enmity arising from patience.

FRIENDS.

That Paracu-ráma, by whom the earth was made destitute of warriors time after time, and by whom deeds of matchless power and courage are done, is heard.

RÁMA.

What! is the high-mindedness of Paracu-ráma, trea-

* *i.e.*, Skanda, the god of war.

sure of great learning, contracted all at once? He who, after making the quarters of the world to have their monarchs, like forests of bamboos, uprooted thrice seven times by the strength of his arm, which is praiseworthy for his victory over the famed Kártikeya, then gave the earth with its islands to his teacher Kacyapa in the horse-sacrifice; and dwelling in a region given up by the ocean, which was driven back by his arms, performs penance.

(*Behind the scenes a voice is heard.*)

The saint, descendant of Bhrigu, regarded with pain and glances of fear by the chamberlains, grieved at the decay of their strength, and whose faces are made awry by this obstacle to their sight, pursues his way unhindered; and bent upon finding Ráma, and filled with anger, enters, alas! the chamber of the princess, while cries of lamentation are sent forth by the domestics.

RÁMA.

Surely these are the guides to the path of good behaviour; how is it, then, that this wise man behaves so rashly? Let it be, I will approach.

[*He walks round proudly and haughtily.*

FRIENDS.

The women's chambers are filled with lamentations of all the domestics, terrified, and alarmed, and uttering cries on all hands: "Alas! divine, moon-faced Rámachandra! O son-in-law!" Therefore, O princess, tell this to the prince.

SÍTÁ.

Then let us hasten, and speak to the prince, who is gone forth with speed.

[*So saying she walks round.*

FRIENDS.

Prince, Prince, look at the Princess, whose quick gait is tremulous, and rendered uneven with haste.

RÁMA (*turning back with affection and tremor*).

Surely you at least ought to detain this timorous one!

FRIENDS.

Friend, friend, thou with the flush of love spread over thy lotus-like face, filled with the beauty of thy lily-like eyes glancing and open, ever in our presence wouldst describe this Ráma as able to destroy gods and demons, as the happiness of the three worlds, as having the mark of the fortune of great victory. Therefore how comes it that when the prince turns his face towards victory thou art affrighted?

SÍTÁ.

Because of Paracu-ráma, who brings woe to all Kshatriyas.

[*She shows signs of fear, &c.*

RÁMA.

Darling, return with good cheer.

(*A voice behind the scenes.*)

O fugitives! where is Ráma, son of Dacaratha?

WOMEN.

Alas, alas! 'tis his name and none other that he utters.

RÁMA.

This sound of the voice, strong as the peal of terrible thunder-clouds clashing against each other, of him whose action is violent with haste, which well becomes him, pleases the hollow of my ear.

[*Thus speaking he walks round.*

SÍTÁ.

What help is there? (*holding him by his bow.*) O prince! you must not indeed go until our father comes.

FRIENDS.

Shame is revealed by our dear friend with another feeling.

RÁMA (*speaking to himself*).

Love conquers. (*Aloud.*) Then I will leave my bow and go.

(*Behind the scenes he repeats*)—O fugitives, &c.

SÍTÁ.

Then I will detain you by force.

RÁMA.

Alas! alas! Through the coming of one who is proud, and who is a treasure of penance and valour, love for the company of the good and anger at the violence of a hero drag me on the one side, and on the other the embrace of Vaidehí, ever stealing my mind, pleasing and cool as sandal, the moon, and dew, hinders me.

FRIENDS.

That Paracu-ráma is indeed come, bearing his axe, very sharp, flashing, gleaming with the bright motion of his body seen in the light of the flaming sun, and wearing locks of hair which resemble thousands of flames of fire burning, and shooting upwards; by whom the earth is shaken with the fierce blow of his staff, huge and massive, being torn by the distant east,—that demon to all Kshatriyas.

RÁMA.

Here is the descendant of Bhrigu, the only warrior in the three worlds and a saint; who, like a great mass of splendours, cannot easily be approached, like the union of majesty and penance endowed with a bright form, and like the fierce warrior spirit reduced to a solid form. (*With surprise.*) Although holy yet terrible in action, a storehouse of vows, powerful beyond measure, wearing a form pleasing and yet awful, he shines like the Átharvana Veda; for he is the essence of power solidified, starting up in the individual, disguised as a Bráhman, capable of destroying the entire collection of worlds, of a fierce spirit;—that essence of power of the god of gods, who conquered Tripura, who is roused to wrath, assuming the form of Kála, Rudra, and Fire, appropriate to the destruction of the world. Oh, the wondrous self-action of the divine one! His axe surrounded with sheets of bright flames is near; on his shoulder is a quiver; and on his body matted locks, a bow, bark-clothing, and a deer-skin; an arrow flashes in his hand, in which a string of nuts forming a bracelet revolves; his dress spreads a twofold splendour, terrible and peaceful.

Dear one! he is our superior, therefore turn aside and veil yourself.

SÍTÁ.

Alas! alas! he is indeed come. (*Joining her hands together.*) O noble one! defend me. Dear but rash prince! be gracious to me.

RÁMA.

Ah, dear one! he is a saint, and besides a great warrior; therefore 'tis pleasing to me. Let thy trembling cease, O timorous one! Thou art a Kshatriya, I am a Kshatriya, descended from Raghu, able to confront him, whose fame is widely spread in the world, and whose arm itches with pride.

Enter JÁMADAGNYA.

JÁMADAGNYA (*in anger*).

Oh, the self-ignorance of an evil-minded warrior boy! Though indeed he felt no fear of the god who is the husband of Bhavání, and whose soul is tranquil by the greatness of his mercy to all creatures, when he broke his bow; still had he not heard of his son Skanda, or of me, his pupil dear as Skanda? This is the change to harshness of me who am otherwise tranquil; because sovereignty once more abides with Kshatriyas, and by them alone bows are now borne, and haughty deeds of them who pride in the strength of their arms I now again hear of with pain.

RÁMA.

When the saint, the greatness of whose penance, splendour, and prowess cannot be told, and who is a treasury of penance, incited with not undue pride attacks me in anger, then my hand with excitement throbs for the act worthy of the pride which arises from recent instruction in the bow, and also to embrace his feet. But he is not an object for such respect.

JÁMADAGNYA.

O fugitives! where is Ráma, son of Dacaratha?

RÁMA.

I am here, here, sir.

JÁMADAGNYA.

Good, O Prince, good! Truly thou art indeed a descendant of Ikshváku. Thou, whose nature is pure by birth, offerest thyself through pride to me, who am seeking thee for destruction; just as the royal young of a wild elephant offers itself to the foe of beasts,* whose paw, like a thunderbolt, cleaves the hammer-like temples of elephants.

WOMEN.

May the sin be pardoned, and the evil omen averted.

JÁMADAGNYA (*beholding him and speaking to himself*).

This pleasant one became the son of a Kshatriya. This youth, who possesses a form encircled by tufts of hair five in number and moving, beautiful and noble, grand and pleasing to the mind, and bearing marks of

* The lion.

natural good fortune, even the moment he is seen carries away my mind by the glory of his passing beauty; still he must indeed be killed. Alas! for the cruelty of the vow of warriors! (*Aloud.*) Let the axe, wielded by the stalwart arm of the descendant of Bhrigu, fearful and incited by anger arising from the act of breaking the bow of the glorious Civa, an act unheard of aforetime, flaming and strong, be for a moment the guest of thy broad throat; that axe by which the god Civa is celebrated in the world as the god of the keen-edged axe.

WOMEN.

Alas! alas! he is indeed excited.

RÁMA (*beholding him with firmness, respect, and curiosity*).

This is that axe which it is said was granted of old by the purple-throated god, pleased by the victory over Skanda and his followers, as a favour to thee, his pupil for a thousand years.

FRIENDS.

O Princess! look! The Prince, whose self-confidence is rising up and filling the soul, by reason of his freedom from fear and his firm courage smiles at the receipt of the weapon from Civa.

[SÍTÁ *looks with surprise and tears.*

JÁMADAGNYA (*to himself*).

A marvel! a marvel! His manner is indeed different; and this his good nature, which utters words the meaning of which I cannot fully understand, is beyond praise;

and so is his goodness, and his courageous self-reliance is grand and noble by reason of his pride. (*Aloud.*) O Ráma! son of Dacaratha, here is that very axe, dear to my venerable teacher.

FRIENDS.

His conversation is as of one taking breath for a moment.

JÁMADAGNYA.

The god of war, well practised in the use of weapons, although surrounded by hosts of divine warriors, was indeed vanquished by me. Pleased even by such an act, my revered tutor who loves merit embraced me and gave me this axe.

RÁMA (*to himself*).

Why does he say, "by such an act?" Oh, the greatness of his haughty pride! (*Aloud.*) And for this, O saint, thy fame as a warrior is spread in heaven and earth. That weapon, by which alone the holy but wrathful instructor, the husband of Chandí, attained renown in the three worlds, as the god of the keen-edged axe; by that, won in the victory over the enemy of Táraka, thy fame as Ráma of the axe has attained splendour. Besides, thy birth is from Jamadagni; that revered god who bears the bow pináka* is thy teacher; but thy valour is not in the range of speech, nor can it be fully revealed by acts; and thy liberality extends to the free gift of the earth surrounded by its seven oceans. What is there of your majesty—a storehouse of truth, sacred learning, and penance—that is not most excellent in the world?

* The peculiar weapon of Civa.

FRIENDS.

The noble prince knows language pleasing to the saint.

JÁMADAGNYA.

Ráma! Ráma! endowed with a form pleasing to the eye and like to thy mind, whose welcome virtues are beyond thought, thou dost captivate my heart in all manner of ways.

Moreover, my chest, which is like a wall torn up by the grinding teeth of Heramba, and which is marked with scars from the arrows of the war-god, and which is covered with bristling hair as with a coat of mail, from meeting with a surpassing warrior desires to embrace thee. I speak the truth.

FRIENDS.

O Princess! see the good fortune of your husband. But you do yourself wrong in always turning your face aside.

[SÍTÁ *sighs and sheds tears.*

RÁMA.

Sire, the word embrace is at variance with your present behaviour.

FRIENDS.

The modesty of the brave and noble hero is made resplendent by his high-mindedness.

JÁMADAGNYA (*to himself*).

Oh! the mind of this warrior-prince perceives the ripe excellence of the merits of himself and others, and is pure by his noble birth; but his great pride, which is hardly seen by reason of exceeding courtesy, may be perceived by one of skilful judgment. Though he is attracted by the marvellous acts of me who am no common hero, excelling, as I do, all in brave deeds; still he exhibits indifference towards me; therefore, he is some great being wearing the form of a warrior boy, made of a number of excellences, and high-mindedness surpassing belief. A wonder! we cannot but infer that his form possesses countless holy qualities, consisting in the welcome gift of protection to the worlds; for in him there shine both beauty and splendour, made brighter by his natural good qualities, and holiness and self-respect, and victory and prowess. For he is the science of war changed and possessing a body, in order to protect the worlds; the duty of heroes endowed with a form to guard the treasure of sacred lore, like a collection of efficient causes, or an assemblage of good qualities, or a heap of holy actions in the world, existing in a visible state. (*Aloud.*) O ladies! let this woman enter into the house.

RÁMA (*to himself*).

So be it.

(*Behind the scenes a voice is heard.*)

Síradhvaja with bow in hand comes here indeed; and Catánanda descendant of Gotama, the family priest of the Janakas.

FRIENDS.

O Princess! your father is indeed come. Let us go into the house.

SÍTÁ (*to herself*).

Divine goddess of war! I join my hands in prayer to thee.

[*The women retire.*

JÁMADAGNYA.

This is that wise king Janaka, guarded by Angiras his family priest, to whom the saint Yájnavalkya, pupil of the sun, revealed the highest sacred learning. He leads a good life; still the thought that he is a Kshatriya causes me a headache, and rouses my anger.

Enter JANAKA *and* CATÁNANDA.

CATÁNANDA (*in an excited manner*).

O king! what is proper in this case?

JANAKA.

Sire, if this saint be a guest, let a seat, and water for the feet, and water for the hands be got ready for the holy man; and after that the meat-offering. But if without any reason he is a foe, and hates us in the matter of our son; then the bow must control him, void as he is of courtesy.

[*They walk round.*

RÁMA.

How is it, noble Sir, that you shed such tears?

JÁMADAGNYA.

'Tis nothing. As soon as thou arrivest within the range of my sight, happiness coming in full force attains exceeding greatness, and the pleasure of the eye enhances its delight; still thou who art only a young bridegroom though glorious and pleasing to my heart, must be slain because thou hast insulted my teacher. At the thought of this I have long been suffering pain.

RÁMA.

O Bhárgava! I know thou dost pity me.

JÁMADAGNYA.

But thinkest thou that thou art protected? The axe shall fall on thy neck, though thy neck resembles a shell, and thy body shines like a cloud charged with nectar.

RÁMA.

Truly indeed thou art prevented by pity (from harming me).

JÁMADAGNYA.

Ah! even upon me he scowls. Ah! Kshatriya boy! thou art but a child, and newly married to a wife; at the thought of this I feel such pain as I never did aforetime. This report is well known, and it is thus sung in the world, that Ráma son of Jamadagni cut off the head of his mother with his own hand.

Besides, O fool! known indeed by all creatures is my nature, who am ever tearing from the womb and cutting into pieces even unborn babes, from my anger towards the descendants of Kshatriyas; and who am filled with pride, and subdue on every hand the families of Kshatriyas, even to twenty-one times, and make the fire-like anger of my sire burn lower by reason of his great delight arising from death-offerings of pools filled with their blood.

RÁMA.

In thy words there is the human vice of cruelty. What boast can there be of that?

JÁMADAGNYA.

Ah! Kshatriya boy! thou art very bold. Strike, bend the bow, I wish to receive the first stroke. For if I deal the blow, what canst thou do with the next?—thou, a headless trunk, whose hard chest is severed in two by the axe, which glitters with the shooting forth of fire that spreads around with hisses.

JANAKA *and* CATÁNANDA.

Son Rámabhadra! stay in security.

RÁMA.

Alas! I am become dependent on the command of another.

JÁMADAGNYA.

I hope Angirasa is well.

CATÁNANDA.

Most assuredly after seeing thee. Besides, if thou art our highly-esteemed guest, then we have prepared what is meet for guests.

JÁMADAGNYA.

A family priest, of well-spent life, learned, a householder, the pupil of Yájńavalkya,—towards him everything is due; but I seek not the condition of a guest.

CATÁNANDA.

Thou didst indecently enter the women's apartments, whereby our propriety was outraged.

JÁMADAGNYA.

I am a Bráhman, living in a forest, ignorant of the custom that prevails in the houses of the great.

RÁMA (*to himself*).

This excess of arrogance towards kings, shown by him who gave as a present the whole world, looks well indeed.

JANAKA.

How is it that thou dost plot a sinful act against the young descendant of Raghu who is under our protection?

Enter a CHAMBERMAID.

O King! the ladies are met together to unloose the marriage thread: let the bridegroom be sent.

JANAKA *and* CATÁNANDA.

Son Rámabhadra! thy kinsfolk call thee: therefore go.

RÁMA.

O noble Jámadagnya! thus my superiors command.

JÁMADAGNYA.

What blame is there? Let thy duty to the world be done, and let thy kinsfolk see thee. But foresters tarry not long in towns. I wish to go, therefore let no time be wasted.

RÁMA.

Even so.

Enter SUMANTRA.

The much respected Vasishtha and Vicvámitra invite you and the descendant of Bhrigu.

The others.

Where are they?

SUMANTRA.

At the court of the great King Dacaratha.

RÁMA.

At the command of our superiors we go.

[*Exeunt omnes.*

END OF THE SECOND ACT.

ACT III.

Enter VASISHTHA, VICVÁMITRA, JANAKA, *and* CATÁNANDA.

VASISHTHA *and* VICVÁMITRA.

O Jámadagnya! The descendant of Ikshváku, the beloved friend of Indra by reason of his destroying the enemies to the rites of sacrifice and to good works, a hero in whom the earth possesses a king, as the sky possesses a king in the thunder-armed Indra, before whom we exist,—what more can we say? That king of the world bending in entreaty, and loving his son, asks protection of thee. Therefore cease from this fruitless strife, and let this be done.

The heifer is ready for sacrifice, and the food is cooked in ghee. Thou art a learned man come to the house of the learned; favour us." *

* *i.e.*, by staying and participating in the sacrifice.

JÁMADAGNYA.

I beg your pardon;—but I will endure it, if Ráma be not an excellent warrior.* Do you mark. Ráma, though a child, is renowned for his marvellous acts; when Bhárgava met with insult from him, why did Bhárgava, impatient as he is, stand idle? If this be asked, who may know that it was from the respect he had for holy men? There may be one who knows it: but again, there is no one to tell how the case stood; for the conduct of warriors is readily exposed to enmity. Besides, when the fame of the great is got together from all quarters whatever; foul rumour, to which increase is given without reason by the common people, having with difficulty found some ground for tattling, however small, never ceases.

VASISHTHA.

O my son! why carry this demon-like weapon all thy life? Jámadagnya! thou art a learned man, seek then the path that is pure; and besides, thou art a forester, therefore woo the four states of friendship and the like, which give calmness to the mind. Yes, and let the painless mental state called glorious smile on thee; and let it cause thee to lay aside thy axe: from the favour of this state arises wisdom, which is called the truth-bearer, the power of which in all things cannot be attained by external means, which is free from misery and misfortune, which is powerful, and the means of perceiving the inner splendour. For a Bráhman should so live, that he may escape the death of sin: and thou hast

* *The meaning seems to be,*—I will consent to stay if Ráma admits that he cannot contend against me.

entered upon another course. See! This assembly of saints, this aged Yudhájit, and the aged monarch Lomapáda with his ministers, and this king also of the Janakas, unceasing in sacrifice, speaking the Veda, of venerable years, are indeed thy suppliants.

JÁMADAGNYA.

True indeed; but unless I have destroyed my enemies at the root, I cannot bear to see again the glorious Tryambaka my instructor, and my instructress Párvatí.

VIÇVÁMITRA.

If you regard holy teachers, then think of me also. Moreover the three saints, Vasishtha, Bhrigu, and Angiras, that sprang from Hiranyagarbha,—here is Vasishtha, thou art the descendant of Bhrigu, and here is the great grandson of Angiras.

JÁMADAGNYA.

I will make atonement for transgressing against you, since you are worthy of respect; but I will not so dishonour my great vow to wield the weapon. For, since the defence of honour is naturally more welcome even than salvation, see! it is so also in my case. You are kinsmen; but this my arm is rough and marked with scars of the bow-string.

VIÇVÁMITRA (*to himself*).

His speech which at every word declares his high-mindedness worthy of esteem, even while piercing my heart, causes my surprise.

JÁMADAGNYA.

Besides, O revered son of Kucika! Assuredly the noble Vasishtha has his mind fixed only upon the Supreme; do thou, time-honoured instructor of the conduct of heroes, say when one born in the pure race of Bhrigu has taken up a weapon, what is proper for him in that case?

VASISHTHA (*to himself*).

Truly he is great by his good qualities, but by nature he is a demon; for he is altogether proud from the excellence of his behaviour.

VICVÁMITRA.

Son! I will say this. Thou roused to anger by the outrage done to one person didst make a slaughter of the race of Kshatriyas with a destruction of babes conceived, so as to leave none remaining, eradicating that very race though sprung from the seed of Bráhmans, full twenty-one times; but when restrained by thy aged ancestors Chyavana and others, thou didst cease from thy anger.

JÁMADAGNYA.

I did indeed cease from the great task of the slaughter of the Kshatriyas enjoined by my father's death. What denial is there of that? Did not my axe, sharp as the thunder-bolt, leave the slaughter of the Kshatriyas, pleasant as it was, and cleave firewood and fuel? and the staff-like bow, with its dense arrow-fangs, bears a likeness to a snake from which the fire-like poison is gone. Thus my flaming anger and the axe were restrained by me, at the command of Chyavana and others; so that again in time the quarters of the world were made dense with the great families of kings, as with forests which have sprung up after burning. But Ráma must lose his head for another reason. Then, after I have cut off the head of this child of the Rághavas who has done the wilful deed, and am gone once more to the forest, let the Raghus and Janakas long prosper; but let there not by any means be again so great an outrage.

CATÁNANDA.

Has any one the power to insult even the shade of the king of Videha, a king and saint, an assistant in sacrifice most dear to me? What then of his son-in-law? We here, as the household fire, have in like manner dwelt for a long time in this householder's house, supported by elders of holy action as by pillars. If insult be offered him by another, then shame upon us, and shame upon our priestly state beloved as it is, and shame upon the family of Angiras.

VICVÁMITRA.

Well done! O son, descendant of Gotama, well done! This King Síradhvaja has maintained his honour through thee his family priest. The realm of that king, to whom thou a learned Bráhman art the family priest guarding the state, suffers no distress, totters not, and does not decay.

JÁMADAGNYA.

Many Kshatriya priests besides thee have felt the divine splendour; but common splendours grow dim before an uncommon glory.

CATÁNANDA (*angrily*).

Thou bull! heinous sinner by the slaughter of the unoffending races of kings! wicked and distorted in act! loathsome in deed! heathen such as none aforetime! base-born warrior! how is it that thou art so bold in this place! What! art thou not a Bráhman indeed! Alas! what behaviour in a great Bráhman! the beheading even of a mother, the cutting to pieces of babes unborn, the slaughter of kings engaged in sacrifice heinous as the killing of a Bráhman!

JÁMADAGNYA.

Ah! speaker of good words! vile, vile priest to petty kings! thou son of Ahalyá! am I base-born?

CATÁNANDA.

Ah! wicked foul-mouthed one, disgrace to the family of Bhrigu! let these kings and elders long-suffering by reason of their greatness suffer it indeed; but Catánanda will not thus suffer it.

[*Thus speaking he sprinkles water from his water-jar.*

VASISHTHA.

Who is here? let him be pacified. This descendant of Angiras, like a fire fanned by a blow-pipe, fearful by the outpouring in drops of offerings of ghee, possesses the brightness of holiness, terrible as a flaming fire.

CATÁNANDA (*hurriedly taking up the water of cursing*).

Observe, courtiers! I, in my anger, will very soon with violence reduce to ashes him who is arrogant through his destruction of others, and who is assailing you; just as the fire of the lightning scattered by whirling stormy winds reduces a tree to ashes.

(*A voice behind the scenes.*)

Be calm, O sire! let the unapproachable fire of penance be quenched towards one who is come to our house. He is praiseworthy for his good qualities, and the best of Bráhmans, and our own kinsman. Is this conduct proper towards him when he is come to our home? Since he, wise as he is, has strayed from the right path, by this the warrior race is to achieve conquest. Be thou tranquil.

VASISHTHA (*taking away the water of cursing*).

Dear Catánanda! be it as the great King Dacaratha says. Moreover, that great happiness which is beyond words we will meditate upon in our mind. Thou, accompanied by Jávâli and others, shouldst make a peace-offering over the fire. Then for the purpose of victory let the holy Vámadeva, uttering victorious sentences, hymns, and chapters of the Veda, pronounce them with our pupils.

[*He embraces and leaves the stage.*

JÁMADAGNYA.

Mark the loud threats of a boy supported by warriors! But what of him? O Bráhmans! you who live upon the favour of the king of Kosala and Videha, and all you warriors who dwell within the seven islands and heights, we declare, whoever among you here boasts either of his penance or arms, let him unable to bear it behold in me an enemy arrogant with pride. Paracu-ráma will make the earth to be without Ráma, and destitute of Síradhvaja and Dacaratha, and, not content, will destroy their kinsfolk too.

(*A voice behind the scenes.*)

O Bhárgava! Bhárgava! thou art indeed over haughty.

JÁMADAGNYA.

Janaka here forsooth takes offence at our pride, and is excited.

Enter JANAKA.

That glory of warriors, crowned with victory, ours by nature, which reached its zenith through the destruction of enemies, and by the power of old age, and by a constant attention to the performance of household rites, and through the acquisition of a true knowledge of the supreme spirit;—that glory arising hastens once more our bow to action.

JÁMADAGNYA.

O Janaka! thou indeed art sacred and aged, and intent upon holiness—thee, the best of sages pupil of the sun instructed in the Vedánta. If knowing this I approached thee, as is my custom, with courtesy, then why dost thou, knowing no fear, speak hard words in anger?

JANAKA.

His feelings are moved, and courtesy is shown. Thus you hear, O courtiers! He is born in the line of Bhrigu, and he is engaged in penance, as it is well known. Although he hates us, still we have had patience with him for a long time. When again and again he boldly shakes us like a blade of grass, then let the bow be bent against him, although he is a Bráhman. There is no other resource.

JÁMADAGNYA (*with glances of anger and derision*).

What dost thou say? what dost thou say?—"the bow!" 'tis a marvel! Even though beholding the laughter of my scorn, the marks of which are clear as a fire, excited by the sight of Kshatriyas, and though beholding the axe sharpened on the heads of enemies, its whetstone, this kinsman of warriors, filled with pride and falsely elated by the schooling of Yájñavalkya and somewhat decrepit with old age, prates against me.

JANAKA (*hurriedly*).

What more in this matter? Let this bow, the fang-like points of which are huge, surrounded by a tongue-like string; which has a loud roar, deep, awful, and resounding, make its huge hollow to resemble the laughing gape of the engine-like mouth of the God of Death engaged in devouring.

[*Thus speaking he strings his bow.*

(*A voice behind the scenes.*)

Cease, O king and ancient bowman! how does thy hand by which thousands of kine were given away in constant sacrifice, and which is entirely covered with grey hair, touch the arrow against this Bráhman.

JANAKA.

My friènd, great King Dacaratha! Let him in truth insult us, that is nothing. When a Bráhman speaks harsh words, who feels pain of mind? But how is this sinful boy to be borne, when he prates in our ear hard words opposed to the happiness of our son?

JÁMADAGNYA.

Ah! vile-minded outcast of warriors! thou insultest me with the name of boy. Arise! arise! Let the axe by which thy throat, teeth, and neck, falling to pieces, mixed with semen, bones, nerves, sinews, entrails, breast, lungs, and liver, are cut into bits,—the axe which is marked with gouts of foaming blood welling up from the blood-vessels, veins, and neck through the cutting of thy head, cleave thee limb from limb in a horrid heap, just like a beast.

DACARATHA (*coming in between them*).

O Bhárgava! Bhárgava! This king is to us dearer than our own body; by reason of the insolent words spoken to him we suffer pain in every way.

JÁMADAGNYA.

What then?

DACARATHA.

Therefore we will not bear it.

JÁMADAGNYA.

Thou too like another assailant dost attack me. Reflect, I am Ráma the son of Jamadagni, by my very nature ever impatient of obstacles, and you are a Kshatriya.

DACARATHA.

Therefore thou art not lightly regarded. The right of taming those who are hard to be tamed devolves upon Kshatriyas: thou art hard to be tamed, and we are those Kshatriyas who punish. Be still at once; what more must be said? Thou art tamed this moment. Where are Bráhmans intent upon tranquillity, and where is the weapon that is borne by a Kshatriya?

JÁMADAGNYA (*laughing*).

After a long time, methinks, the son of Jamadagni is ruled by a master, since you Kshatriya kings are his guides.

DACARATHA.

What! is there any doubt of this? If a man, either ignorant or meeting with some perplexity or having doubt in his knowledge, commits an act that is opposed to the seen or unseen law; of such an one his teacher is the protector; but if, when there is knowledge free from doubt or perplexity, a man commits a hostile act, and the king punishes him not, then this disorder among the subjects arises.

VICVÁMITRA.

Oh! the great king speaks rightly. If knowledge exists not, or if it is perplexed with doubt, or frustrated, then pay court to the feet of Vasishtha. Surely there is some fault in thy knowledge, else how would there be the utterance of evil words? If in purity thou dost commit a crime, kings will not endure it.

JÁMADAGNYA.

The divine lord is my instructor in duty, holiness, and the bow. How can Kshatriyas teach courtesy to him who destroyed all the Kshatriyas? A relationship with the noble Vasishtha is worthy of respect in the matter of age; but in rivalry there is none superior or equal to me by penance and knowledge.

VASISHTHA.

"Defeat from a descendant of Bhrigu!" the thought is pleasing to us. But mark the violation of the time-honoured custom in our house, which ought to be maintained at least by us, and which is pleasing to us by reason of its excellence.

JANAKA, DACARATHA, *and* VICVÁMITRA.

Ignoble and disrespectful one! thou who art unruly even before Vasishtha, the ancient instructor of the world, shalt be tamed by us by main force * like a wild elephant.

JÁMADAGNYA.

Thus am I shaken. The anger which has long been scorching like a barb driven into the vitals of my heart, formed into a ball and compressed by the weight of inner firmness at the bidding of my elders—that mine anger, since my spirit has been disturbed by words of contempt, now flames up indeed, like the aurva-fire of the ocean, the waters of which are scattered by winds at the end of the age. Ah! this contempt is felt, and the axe like my anger flames. Are the kings on the earth placed in the

* The reading here, I think, ought to be *parákramya*.

might of Dacaratha? Then let even the twenty-second destruction of the Kshatriya race, which will make a festival for the enraged God of Death, and which is terrible as the destruction of the world, take place after a long interval.

VASISHTHA.

Alas! alas! truly he is our kinsman. Still through pride he acts in a terrible manner; how can he escape being killed? If he should be often seen by me, insulted as I am, that would be a wrong to the boy who is descended from Bhrigu.

VICVÁMITRA.

O Jámadagnya! thou regardest me as destitute of Bráhmanical glory in the water of cursing and without skill in the use of weapons. Thou dost slight the assembly of Bráhmans and Kshatriyas, and thou hast a cruel wish towards the boy Ráma; by such a transgression thou dost pain us. Thou art worthy to be protected as a relation. My right hand, trembling with anger, since I am filled with wrath against thee, seeks the water of cursing; and my left hand from its former training seeks the bow.

JÁMADAGNYA.

O Kaucika! if thou dost possess the Bráhmanical glory, or if thou art a bowman by the laws of thy race, come, I will outshine thy penance by my fierce penance. But in the other case let the axe do its duty.

(*A voice behind the scenes.*)

I, Ráma, pupil of Kaucika, make my obeisance here,

and request. I will conquer the enemy of Kárttavírya-Arjuna arrogant by his victory over Paulastya, though he is the conqueror of Kártikeya. Greeting be to you!

DACARATHA.

Rámabhadra is come. What will happen now?

JANAKA.

Oh! 'Tis well. Give the word at once. Let Rámabhadra conquer. He is the punisher of the proud. This warrior is the lord of the worlds. All of us, with Vasishtha as our chief, are surety in this matter.

DACARATHA.

Assuredly this very day is Rámabhadra born in the virtuous house of us, who are sacrificers and whose fame is widely spread, and who have undertaken the vow of protection; since the Bráhmans, who understand the past, present, and future by the brightness of their knowledge, recognise in him, although a mere child, a power that is beyond expression.

JÁMADAGNYA.

Come! O Prince! Thou wilt conquer, I suppose, the son of Jamadagni. (*Smiling.*) Assuredly thou wilt not conquer, for the son of Renuká, thy destroyer, is hard to be vanquished. For now, let the bow terrible with the sound of the bow-string dense and collected in the quarters of the world, perform the act of devouring as the voracious angel of death, with the arrows which make the roaring sound of a fire awful with its uprising flames, and are sprinkled with blood that flows from the cavern-like throats of slaughtered Kshatriyas.

[*Exeunt omnes.*

END OF THE THIRD ACT.

ACT IV.

(*A voice behind the scenes.*)

O deities! may the auspicious acts continue. The holy saint Kaucika, pupil of Kricácva, is victorious. Now the Kshatriya race descended from the sun is victorious in the world. The punisher of the enemy of Kshatriyas, under the vow of granting protection to the worlds, the refuge of the universe, the moon of the family of the sun, is conqueror.

Enter hurriedly in a heavenly car CÚRPANAKHÁ *and* MÁLYAVÁN.

MÁLYAVÁN.

Child! thou hast seen the unanimous disposition of the gods, that Indra and the rest have become his panegyrists.

CÚRPANAKHÁ.

That which you intended is not effected; and now I tremble with fear. What, therefore, should be done in this case?

MÁLYAVÁN.

That queen who had two boons formerly granted to her by King Dacaratha, the mother of Bharata by name

Kaikeyí,—her handmaid named Manthará, who brings the tidings to Dacaratha, has been sent from Ayodhyá to Mithilá, and is now in the neighbourhood of Mithilá; so I have very lately been told by spies. Do thou enter her body and act as I tell thee.

[*He whispers in her ear.*

CÚRPANAKHÁ.

What will my poor powers effect in this way?

MÁLYAVÁN.

Our bad designs would be frustrated in the house of Ikshváku, especially against such a conqueror.

CÚRPANAKHÁ.

What then?

MÁLYAVÁN.

Then by the plea of practising meditation when we have allured him to a great distance and brought him to the presence of the demons, while, ignorant of the country, he wanders about in the huge forests of the Vindhya mountain, our attacks will be easily made. For Virádha, Danukabandha, and others will roam about, hostile to the sacrifices in the Dandaka forest. When, indeed, his power as a chief is taken away, his power of energy may be baffled by guile; and the capture of Sítá by Rávana must not be prevented, and that will be easy in this way, and advantageous.

CÚRPANAKHÁ.

But he may derive some advantage from the companionship of Lakshmana.

MÁLYAVÁN.

As Ráma must be considered a hero perfect in the science of arms, so too must he. But covert punishment can be used as effectually against two as against one.

ÇÚRPANAKHÁ.

To me these two things seem not proper. The bringing near of the son of Daçaratha, who is now afar off; and the quarrel about a woman, which never can be made good, with him who has no quarrel against us.

MÁLYAVÁN.

Why! He is indeed near since there is no interval of territory between us. But how can the destroyer of the sons of Sunda and Upasunda with their followers, and the enemy of Tátaká, have no quarrel with us. And how can the enmity of Ráma and Rávana be beyond remedy? See! the world is to be guarded by him, but we are ever doing violence to the world: when this is the case, what conciliation can there be with him whose actions are unfriendly, and whose mind is hostile to us? What things are there that the descendant of Raghu desires, since he has been chosen by the gods as their lord? Therefore, bribery holds not in this case, nor yet must dissension be the means employed by you against him, and even the infliction of punishment, if it be open, seems not well against a superior enemy. But punishment must be inflicted secretly, and this is the commencement of it. Since this is so, what else should he do but carry off Sítá? Moreover, if he whose wife has been carried off by the enemy is filled with shame, he merely takes refuge in a form of death. He who is crushed down, and is destitute of majesty, is dead indeed; or else, after suffering pain, he joins in a treaty. If he should rise up to destroy us with anger made fierce by the outrage, the ocean will not be able to obstruct his onward course; for he is a hero equal to the sun in power. But the enemy will be slain by the terrible monkey, the son of the thunder-bearer, whose power is awful and whose friendship with Rávana was secured aforetime; and by this alliance much will be effected.

ÇÚRPANAKHA.

What?

MÁLYAVÁN.

Child! thou art fond of Rávana, and thou knowest his affairs, therefore the pain of my heart is told without fear. Ráma, who is ever doing us evil and who is our oppressor as there is no interval of territory between us, is in two ways our enemy; being by nature well governed, and being a Kshatriya. My third grandson, the brother of the lord of night-stalkers, and his enemy, fills me with fear from his extreme nearness to him, just as a serpent. But Kumbhakarna though he lives is like one who lives not, from his propensity to sleep and his want of courtesy; while Vibhíshana, who is endowed with good qualities and a mind versed in sacred lore, has won the attachment of the subjects. But Khara, Dúshana, and Triciras, whose conduct is like that of the family, stand by the king because they obtain wealth from the king, just as people get milk from a cow by means of the calf. And the subjects are disaffected and conspire together. Therefore the royal family, split up with internal dissension will be vanquished by Ráma the moment it is attacked. As it is said, "a cause of calamity however small is easily brought about against one who is attacked." And the remedy for this is to restrain Vibhíshana; but this may be either open punishment, or secret punishment, imprisonment, or banishment. But how would the Rákshasas who are unbroken in their attachment bear his public punishment? Even his punishment in secret, which would be guessed by the wise, would have a bad end, when Ráma who causes the anger of the citizens is the aggressor. If, after he has been defeated, his imprisonment is determined upon, then Khara and the rest from their great friendship for him will change sides; and even if he is banished they will attend him; therefore Khara and the rest must chiefly be thought of. In this lies Ráma's advantage.

CÚRPANAKHÁ.

Alas! the dishonour of dependency! since, although the family tie of Rávana, Khara, and others is equal, our grandfather thinks thus.

MÁLYAVÁN.

Such is the behaviour of the sons of our race.

CÚRPANAKHÁ.

Without Khara and his adherents, how will Vibhíshana act?

MÁLYAVÁN.

He is wise indeed, and on perceiving a change in Rávana he would go into voluntary exile, and we may look on with indifference, and need not think he has any innate fear; since he, whose friendship with Sugríva is deeply rooted even from childhood, would assuredly resort to him whose dwelling is on Rishyamúka, the portion of the prince, a parcel of land given by Válí as a favour; and therefore Válí will rouse himself to action, but not on his resorting to Ráma; though perhaps on his union with Ráma, Válí will not look on with indifference.

CÚRPANAKHÁ.

Then Ráma will kill Válí whose enmity is caused by his victory over Paracuráma, and afterwards the union of Ráma and Vibhíshana will be a calamity; so I think.

MÁLYAVÁN.

Truly, child, he who kills Válí is able to kill us without a doubt; but in that destruction of all may he at least live to continue our race. To him let Ráma, all holy as he is, grant the kingdom.

CÚRPANAKHÁ (*weeping*).

Thus at least let it be.

MÁLYAVÁN.

Go now, child, where thou wast sent; and the performance will be easy, when Vasishtha and Vicvámitra are not near Janaka and Dacaratha. I too will go even to Lanká.

CÚRPANAKHÁ.

Alas ! Mother ! by thee too anguish must be felt.

MÁLYAVÁN.

Alas ! Khara, Dúshana, and the rest, my children ! wretch that I am, you must be slain ! Alas ! my child Vibhíshana ! thou too must be discarded by reason of my interests. Alas ! my darling child Rávana ! I see great distress for thee. My daughter Kaikasí, alas ! thou art undone ! not long wilt thou behold three sons.

[*Exeunt.*

END OF THE VISHKAMBHAKA.

Enter JANAKA *and* DACARATHA *with* VASISHTHA *and* VICVÁMITRA (*the kings embrace*).

JANAKA.

O king ! By the grace of God thou dost prosper, since thou hast such a son as Rámabhadra. The astonishing acts of that great hero which are uncommon and abound with good qualities and surpass the world, and are attended with great success in their results, confer happiness not only upon us but upon the three worlds.

VASISHTHA (*after embracing* VICVÁMITRA).

My friend, descendant of Kucika ! The possession of Ráma's greatness cannot be hoped for even by us, since it is through him that we and the worlds are made contented.

VICVÁMITRA.

This greatness has for its cause the ripening of excellent holiness. What have we to do with so great a pleasure ?

DACARATHA.

Holy descendant of Kucika! speak not so indeed; since former kings, Dilípa and others, descended from the sun, resorted in worship to the all-glorious saint, the husband of Arundhatí, as to the patron goddess of their family; and since the blessings of saints, whose penance is great and whose blessings are true, are attended with praiseworthy results,—even of those blessings this only is the happy cause, namely, that your majesty was pleased with us.

VASISHTHA.

True, such is Vicvámitra. The penance which passes beyond the range of speech and thought, and which is of supreme excellence, kindled with splendours and infinite in extent, shines in this holy saint who can hardly be approached.

VICVÁMITRA.

Holy son of Mitra and Varuna! The Sanatkumára and Angiras are great in learning and penance. If thou dost praise me, then am I as thou sayest indeed; for thy words are truthful. But in the case of Rámabhadra this is no wonder, for the great king Dacaratha is his father. Kings in the race of Manu son of the sun, who are like a visible collection of holy actions, protect their subjects by laws which thou hast proposed. Among those who were most famous in the race and whose actions are holy, he is chief, a warrior, the most excellent of Kshatriyas, a mine of good qualities, the praiseworthy king of earth. Indra moreover, that lord of the worlds who was unscathed in the act of destroying the son of Tvastri, the slayer of Jambha, the ruler of the company of Maruts, selected in many battles this hero who conquers armies, and who ever destroys the demons. How can he, who is of such a character, beget a son of a different character? How can there be surprise herein? The ten-headed chief who conquered the bright god who rules the Maruts, was himself conquered in war by the king who is the ruler of the Haihayas: his destroyer, whose fame was spread abroad in the three worlds, a mighty hero, was vanquished by our boy. What then is left unconquered by him?

ÇADARATHA.

How comes it then that the world is divided between two opinions?

VIÇVÁMITRA.

The boy Rámabhadra with Jámadagnya is approaching here indeed. He who, shining with the glory of warriors and with victory, and bowed down before the saint who is deserving of respect, and yet exalted by his virtues, wearing shame before the chief of the Bhrigus who is reft of the pride of valour, seems like a boy who has committed his first offence against his teacher.

Enter RÁMA *and* JÁMADAGNYA.

RÁMA.

In that by my destiny I violated courtesy towards thee whose venerable feet are attended by holy men who speak the Veda, and who art a mine of learning, penance, and vows, the best of ascetics: do thou, sire, pardon me. I join my hands to thee in entreaty.

JÁMADAGNYA.

No offence, child, was committed towards Jámadagnya, but a service was rendered. The malady of pride, one in number yet in reality a forest of countless vices,—which alone robbed me of my Bráhmanical birth, the virtues of my race, my learning, and good behaviour, and stole away my understanding too,—that was cured for my welfare by thee, O child! dear as thou art to me and kind to Bráhmans.

RÁMA.

How was no offence committed by me, when my wickedness reached so high a pitch that I took up a weapon?

JÁMADAGNYA.

This is your reasoning. Just as a physician is endured, so is a king with a weapon in his hand, in order to eradicate a defect in men which cannot otherwise be remedied.

RÁMA.

Who am I that I should speak and reply to your holiness? Therefore go there, sire.

JÁMADAGNYA.

Where, child, must I go?

RÁMA.

Where my father is, and my sire, Janaka. Perhaps 'tis forgiven. Or where the saints Vicvámitra and Kauçika are.

JÁMADAGNYA.

This now is impossible; and the order of kings must not be transgressed. (*After walking round*). O honoured ones! this Ráma from his pleasantness is not fierce, and yet he is fierce in his valour; since he has inflicted even upon Paracuráma the chastisement of victory.

KINGS.

This expression of good-nature is very noble.

RÁMA.

Here the act of obeisance is made you by the head of Ráma.

ALL.

Come here, child! [*They embrace him.*

JÁMADAGNYA.

Revered son of Mitra and Varuna! I, the son of Jamadagni, here bowing down, request of you and Kaucika, "Let the spiritual guides appoint for me who have been vanquished by Ráma some expiation to release me from that heinous sin caused by trespass against elders. You alone, O sire, were the first revealer of primeval duty; but Manu and others after receiving that knowledge divided it in many ways in their treatises.

VASISHTHA.

Thou who art born in the house of learned men art sinless; but when thou art uncourteous, we are pained; otherwise we are pleased, for this is the nature of elders. But what is thy happiness, that same is ours; therefore thou art purified.

VICVÁMITRA.

We know thy sin was destroyed by Rámabhadra ; for instructors in holiness declare that the punishment inflicted by a king, just like expiation, is a release from sin. What more has the honoured Vasishtha to order in the presence of kings?

RÁMA.

These are the words of saints by whom holiness was revealed, pleasing, grand, and pure.

DACARATHA.

Revered son of Jamadagni! what else would be purifying to thee who art naturally pure? The sacred stream and fire want not purity from aught else.

JÁMADAGNYA.

O goddess earth! be gracious to me by granting me a cleft (to swallow me up).

JANAKA.

Holy one! If it please thee, purify our palace by entering it without fear; this is a pure seat for your holiness.

JÁMADAGNYA.

Yes, if it please the student of the pupil of the sun, a princely and learned man.

[*All sit down.*

DACARATHA.

You dwell outside any town; we too, through being householders, are occupied with our own matters: therefore, our meeting with you which occurred not aforetime, though wished and longed for by us, has this day happened here at last, in consequence of good actions. And here what praise can there be of thee whose greatness has passed beyond the range of praise? And what can be given to thee who givest away the whole earth? Of what use are attendants to one who is self-controlled, O saint? Still Dacaratha with his sons this day makes submission to thee.

JÁMADAGNYA.

Such is your goodness. When I thus reflect, what surprise can I feel at this? That which the wise call the kindled splendour, that treasure of glories, the bright sun, is the author of your line. What else should be an object of praise? You are those descendants of Ikshváku, sacrificers, kings, and priests of the highest order, whose instructor in holiness is Vasishtha, whose power is beyond measure like the Veda. Again, the bending of the bow of the ruler of the gods which gives completion to the sacrifice of war, the earth which is marked with rows of dwelling and posts planted in the seven islands, houses, the sacred Ganges, the ocean, and other well-known things countless in number proclaim your greatness which is linked with undying fame.

VASISHTHA *and* VICVÁMITRA (*aside*).

This too was taught by the boy.

JÁMADAGNYA.

Rámabhadra, consent to my going to the forest.

VICVÁMITRA.

Allow me also then. An increase of the auspicious

acts arising from the union of the children has taken place in the palaces of Raghu and Janaka. The subjection of the chief of Bhrigus—(*He stops in the middle of the sentence*). And when I have paid homage to the dear child whose greatness is known by the chief of Bhrigus I will go well pleased to my home.

DACARATHA.

My son Rámabhadra! thy revered Kaucika is gone.

VICVÁMITRA (*embracing* RÁMA *with tears*).

I cannot bear to leave thee, fair one! but the constant performance of rites deprives me of my free will; for in the case of those who keep sacrificial fires, the condition of householders is beset with sins that may arise from neglect.

VASISHTHA.

You have free liberty to come and go from house to house.

VICVÁMITRA.

If your holiness agrees with me, then come, we will both go to Siddhácrama. As I go with thee before me, I shall become a worthy guest of the mother of Madhuchhandas.

VASISHTHA.

What! in so small a matter as this, can you not control us?

KINGS.

The meeting of these holy sages is pleasant and pure. Even the enmity of these two who know each other's noble-mindedness, but whose soul is unknown by others, shines brightly. What then can be said of their friendship?

(*A voice behind the scenes.*)

The bride of Ráma here pays homage to the holy teachers.

SAINTS.

Child, daughter of Janaka! when the great fears of the slayer of Vritra are allayed by thy husband a hero courteous and successful, let Cachí with her mind pay thee exceeding homage, a mark of respect to the wife of the best of Kshatriyas.

RÁMA (*to himself*).

It may shortly be so, when the demons are torn up by the roots.

SAINTS.

Welcome! Sit here.

[*They rise up.*

THE OTHERS (*rising up*).

Salutation to you.

JÁMADAGNYA.

Jámadagnya greets your majesties.

VASISHTHA *and* VICVÁMITRA.

May thy tranquillity of mind be firm; and may the inner light shine upon thee; and may thy soul be undisturbed in its holy thoughts.

[*Exeunt.*

JÁMADAGNYA (*walking round a little way and then standing still*).

Rámabhadra, my child! pray come here.

RÁMA (*approaching*).

Give me your commands.

JÁMADAGNYA.

The bow which was borne by me, when wearied with the destruction of the Kshatriyas,—that now attains a state devoid of purpose. But let the axe be employed in cutting fuel and the like. The saints who dwell in numbers on the banks of the holy rivers in the Dandaká forest,—among them the demons who dwell in Lanka are ever wandering for their hurt: in whose destruction the bow which this moment is his (Ráma's), and by means of which authority is implanted in the boy, will be useful.

[*He gives it.*

RÁMA (*bowing*).

I accept your commands.

JÁMADAGNYA (*walking round and shedding tears*).

Prince! return.

[*With these words he leaves the stage.*

RÁMA (*shedding tears*).

The revered Bhárgava is gone. (*Reflecting.*) Then may I by some means or other set out for the Dandaká forest. But how will consent be got from my teachers who are fond of Ráma? Since the chief of Bhrigus has laid aside his weapon, and I am dependent on the will of another, alas! the saints, rich in penance, have been expelled by the cruel demons.

(*A voice behind the scenes.*)

Prince! Prince! She who is named Manthará, the dear friend of thy second mother, is come here from Ayodhyá, desirous to see thee.

RÁMA.

'Tis well; for this sorrow of mind arising from the exile of the young people may be dispelled in her. Therefore, dear Lakshmana, bring her near.

Enter LAKSHMANA *and* CÚRPANAKHÁ *in the disguise of* MANTHARÁ.

CÚRPANAKHÁ.

I am Cúrpanakhá, possessing the form of Manthará. The absence of Vasishtha and Vicvámitra has well happened. Oh! here is Ráma, the warrior youth, the conqueror of Paracu-ráma. (*Looking closely at him.*) Ah! the structure of his body, which by reason of the possession of marks of complete good fortune is pleasant as salve to the eyes, would now again excite the heart of a man who has renounced the pleasures of the world, from having long endured great pain, and would delight it with his valour and brave actions.

RÁMA (*bowing down*).

Manthará! is our mother well?

ÇÚRPANAKHÁ.

She is happy and well. Thy second mother, whose bosom teems with affection, embraces and sends thee word: "O son! I remind thee of the two boons promised aforetime by the great king. Become the bearer of my request in this matter. This is the written message to our father."

LAKSHMANA (*takes it and reads*).

By one boon let the boy Bharata enjoy the fortune of sovereignty. (*To himself.*) How, while the noble Ráma lives, can the request of the kingdom for the noble but young Bharata be made? (*Aloud.*) By the other boon, let Rama without delay go to the Dandaká forest. (*To himself.*) Alas! mother, what hast thou done by requesting the exile of the noble one? (*Aloud.*) And let him wearing bark dress stay in it fourteen years, and let no one follow him save his attendants Sítá and Lakshmana only.

(*To himself.*) Ah, wicked widow! base mother! what hast thou done, wicked one, disregarding the cry of mother which was ever made by the mouths of Bharata, Catrughna, Lakshmana, and the noble Prince?

RÁMA.

Oh, the excellent favour! The command to go even there where my soul longs to go; separation has not happened here, for the youth is my attendant.

LAKSHMANA.

By good fortune, the noble one suffers me to follow him.

RÁMA.

Noble Manthará! I am setting out.

CÚRPANAKHÁ.

Salutation now to the divine world in which such Kalpa trees grow.

[*Exit.*

LAKSHMANA.

Ah! our uncle Yudhájit, accompanied by the noble Bharata, approaches our father.

RÁMA.

'Tis well—but, alas! if I embrace not Bharata, I shall have no courage to go; and yet I cannot bear to behold him pained by grief at our exile.

YUDHÁJIT *and* BHARATA *entering and approaching* DACARATHA.

Sire! Let the request be heard which the citizens with one accord make of you. This, thy son, the keeper of the three Vedas,—in him, the Prince Rámabhadra, we are possessed of a king; and, with the favour of thee, our sovereign, we will go sure of welfare and with our desires fulfilled.

DACARATHA.

Friend Janaka! we are entreated of our subjects who seek the welfare of our dear boy; but Maitrávaruna and Kaucika who are fond of Ráma are not here.

JANAKA.

An act that is well done in their absence will give

pleasure to them; and the divine Vámadeva skilled in rites is here indeed.

DACARATHA.

If it be so, then let the great festival of the victory over Paraçu-ráma be joined to the great festival of inauguration.

RÁMA.

How can this be now?

DACARATHA.

Sumantra! let the vessels for inauguration be brought near; and whatever petition any one has, let his desire be satisfied.

RÁMA (*approaching and bowing*).

I have a request to make.

DACARATHA.

What, child?

RÁMA.

The granting of the two boons that were made, that our second mother earnestly requests of thee this day, O sire! and we desire her pleasure.

DACARATHA.

Truly the Raghus are true to their word. Why, son, dost thou doubt? When thou art a suppliant, who values even her life?

RÁMA.

Dear brother! Repeat the request.

LAKSHMANA (*reads*).

"By one boon, &c."

The others.

What! 'tis some other matter indeed. Alas! we are undone.

[*The king faints.*

RÁMA *and* LAKSHMANA.

Father, take heart.

JANAKA.

How can the lady, noble as she is, born in that spotless race of kings, and wife of a monarch who is the pride of the Ikshváku line, commit such a demon-like and monstrous act? Alas! 'tis a great surprise to us.

RÁMA.

Father! father! If you are true to your word, and if Ráma is dear to you, then let our father favour us and let our second mother have her wish fulfilled.

DACARATHA.

Let it be so. What help is there?

JANAKA.

Ah! child Rámabhadra! ah! child Lakshmana! the vow of a forest life, which is worn by the Ikshvákus when old, and after their wealth has been given to their sons,—that thou assumest when only a suckling. Child Jánakí! thou art happy, since the order to accompany thy husband is given by thy elders.

DACARATHA.

Alas! daughter Jánakí, while but a bride, thou art brought as an offering to the demons.

[*Both faint.*

RÁMA.

Our elders are much afflicted: how comes it?

LAKSHMANA.

Such is the force of love and pity that comes upon them. What can be done here? Delay has been forbidden us by the mother of Bharata. Away with the pain of excessive affection.

RÁMA.

Good! oh, thou who art stern in thy purpose! good! The power of thy mind seems not human. Therefore, dear brother, bring Vaidehí.

[*Exit Lakshmana.*

BHARATA.

Uncle! This is becoming your house.

YUDHÁJIT.

Child! I am driven mad. The king enters the mouth of death; these two sons enter the forest; the unhappy bride is given like an offering to the demons; the world is without support; our noble family is ruined by infamy; the wickedness of my sister weakens the whole world.

Enter LAKSHMANA *and* SÍTÁ.

PRINCE.

Prince! Here is the noble lady.

RÁMA.

Come here. (*Passing with* SÍTÁ *and* LAKSHMANA *to the right of the company of elders.*) Uncle! Our father here, and father-in-law, and mothers with their dear children, ought to be comforted in this sorrow by you alone. We are going.

[*He then walks round.*

YUDHÁJIT (*hurriedly*).

How am I to leave him in the forest?

[*He rises up and runs after.*

BHARATA (*following*).

Uncle! Say, what am I to do now?

YUDHÁJIT.

Rámabhadra! Wait for Bharata, thy forest follower, and attendant upon thy feet.

RÁMA.

Truly he too has received the command of the elders to protect the four classes and orders.

BHARATA.

Let that be the task of Lakshmana or Catrughna.

RÁMA.

What! has any one his own choice in this matter?

BHARATA.

Such is my own wish.

RÁMA.

Alas! Is it possible, while I am living, for thee or any other to transgress propriety?

BHARATA.

Alas! how am I abandoned, unhappy one that I am!

[*He faints.*

YUDHÁJIT.

Son! be comforted.

BHARATA (*reviving*).

Uncle! uncle! support me.

YUDHÁJIT.

Son! I do so. (*After whispering in the ear of Bharata.*) O Rámabhadra! He makes this request, "Let the noble one grant me as a favour that pair of golden shoes which were sent by the saint Carabhanga.

RÁMA (*taking them off*).

Receive them, dear brother!

BHARATA (*placing them on his head*).

Noble one!

RÁMA (*embracing him*).

Return with the covering of my feet. Now revive our fathers who have been long in a swoon.

BHARATA.

I now, after performing the inauguration upon the shoes of the noble one, wearing matted hair in Nandigráma, will govern the earth until the noble one returns.

[*He goes to the right of Sítá and Ráma.*

LAKSHMANA.

Noble Bharata! Lakshmana bows to thee.

[*Bharata embraces him, and tries to suppress his tears.*

RÁMA.

Brother! revive our fathers.

BHARATA.

Alas! they do not yet recover.

[*He fans them.*

JANAKA (*recovering and looking round*).

Alas! I am bereaved.

DACARATHA (*reviving*).

Child Rámabhadra! do not go. My life is sinking; I am surrounded by darkness on every side. Sickness such as never before comes upon me and pierces my vitals. Place thy moon-like face near my eyes, and speak a word to me. Ah son! be not thus suddenly unfeeling towards me. Alas! where shall I go? unhappy man that I am!

[*Tottering, and led by Bharata and Janaka, he retires.*

YUDHÁJIT.

Son Rámabhadra! The city slowly collecting in a body, though possessed of many functions, yet combined in one act, with cries of lamentation sent forth here and there, and with its men and women distracted, and asking "What is the matter?"—thus that illustrious city is seen to have suddenly changed, and in it there is a murky day, and the roads are miry with showers of falling tears.

RÁMA.

Uncle! uncle! return. Here is Bharata at your hand.

YUDHÁJIT.

Follow close by me.

RÁMA.

Peace! You are elders and not followers. The command of my mother is that I go with only two attendants.

YUDHÁJIT.

What! Am I the only one following? There are also the citizens with their children and old men; seest thou not? These great Bráhmans, with the sacrificial vessels placed upon their shoulders, come to screen from thee the sun's rays, with their umbrellas obtained for the Vájapeya sacrifice. Here the inhabitants of Saketa, with the sacred fires borne by their wives who are following, and with the sacrificial cows sent on in advance, accompanied by the troops run after thee, old as they are.

RÁMA.

Uncle! uncle! It is the duty of elders alone to keep children from a violation of duty; therefore, oblige us. Return and take back this large concourse of people.

[*Thus speaking he bows.*

YUDHÁJIT.

Child! arise, arise! I here, seeing that I have deceived

you my subjects, will go somewhere, wretched man that I am. To thee Lakshmana of the strong arm! to thee daughter of Vaideha! I bid farewell. I return, wicked man that I am. May fortune attend you.

(*Returning weeping.*) Oh! assuredly the greatness * of this noble behaviour, which will be sung by creatures in every age in the morning, will give purity to the worlds.

[*Exit.*

LAKSHMANA.

Guha, the king of Nishádas, inhabitant of Cringavera, has reported to my noble brother the wicked attempts of the demon Virádha, who has invaded the confines of his realm.

RÁMA.

Therefore, in order to destroy the wicked Virádha, we will go to the mountain Chitrakúta, in the neighbourhood of which is the sacred confluence, and which has its slope purified by the river Mandákiní flowing upon it, and has waters frequented by saints; and, after slaying the demons, and reaching Dandaká, we will proceed to Janasthána, where dwells the King of Vultures.

[*Exeunt omnes.*

END OF THE FOURTH ACT.

* The reading is doubtful. If *Vañjiká* is taken, the meaning is "deception," *i.e.*, concealing from the people Ráma's exile.

ACT V.

Enter SAMPÁTI.

Assuredly to-day the dear Jatáyu approaches our home in the caverns of the Malaya mountain; for the flapping of huge wings, in the expansion and contraction of which the quarters of the sky are for a moment seen and then in turn lost to view; by which the quivering lightning, vivid and shaken, is caused to leave the clouds which are made like snow; by which the tall lines of huge rocks are made to resound, and are scattered on all sides, proclaims aloud the coming of the son of Cyení. The lower world is filled with the furious wind that rushes through the chasms of the ocean from which the hidden fire is tossed up to a distance, and the waters of which are broken and surge upwards; and frightful with the terrible sound that issues loudly from the cavern-like throat of the boar of Vishnu, it roars like a thunder-cloud in the night of the deluge suddenly come.

Enter JATÁYU.

JATÁYU.

I will alight from the sky on a lone peak of the Malaya mountain the base of which is encircled by the river Káverí; where dwells the noble bird descended from Kacyapa, like a second huge mountain which has lost its wings. Pain from the weariness of flying, which takes hold of and makes my wings to droop, has seized upon me: truly the might of all-powerful time, which is called old age, is a cause of impediment to all other powers. Here then is the noble Sampáti, the ancient vulture-king of past ages. Oh, brotherly love! In a past age, when the sun was scorching my limbs from its extreme nearness which happened in our play, as we were practising distant flights; he, thinking I was but young, spread out his wings above me to shield me; and with his own wings protected me altogether from being burned in his compassion.

(*Approaching.*) Noble Kácyapa! Jatáyu greets thee.

SAMPÁTI.

Come hither, child! Cyení is possessed of a son in thee, the ruler of vultures, just as our grandmother Vinatá is in the hero Garutman. (*After embracing.*) Child Jatáyu! is the sorrow Rámabhadra feels at his father's death lessened by the lapse of time?

JATÁYU.

His union with those who are old in learning and penance, and his own firmness, and the just office of protecting, dispel his pain of mind.

SAMPÁTI.

It is reported to me, by the vultures sated with the flesh of Virádha, that Ráma went from Chitrakúta to the hermitage of Carabhanga; and then Carabhanga made an offering of his body in the fire; after that, Ráma visited the saints also,—Sutíkshna and the rest.

JATÁYU.

True, Ráma now at the command of Agastya dwells in Pańchavatí.

SAMPÁTI (*remembering after awhile*).

Ah! there is in Janasthána a place on the banks of the Godávarí named Pańchavatí. Child Jatáyu! the multiplicity of objects and the lapse of time rob me of my memory. In the beginning of the age my knowledge of places went as far as where the foot of Vishnu rose in the sky, having for its banner the beautiful Ganges; and along the borders where the mountain Lokáloka, the bracelet-like boundary of splendours, incloses the seventh ocean.

JATÁYU.

Thither once came Cúrpanakhá loving the son of Raghu.

SAMPÁTI.

Alas! the want of shame! She who living in many centuries had now numbered her thirteenth age, felt no shame while she put to shame that boy who was but a suckling.

JATÁYU.

And by cutting off her ears, nose, and lips, Lakshmana obtained as it were the fame of offering an insult to the ten-headed one.

SÁMPATI.

Then, as the result of that, an attack was commencod by the others.

JATÁYU.

True, and by Rámabhadra alone, fourteen thousand and fourteen demons besides the three, Dúshana, Khara, and Trimúrddhan, were slain in the battle.

SAMPÁTI.

It is a marvel, or perhaps this is no marvel in the case of Dácarathi. But I am perplexed when I think that the great door of enmity is again opened; therefore, child Jatáyu! thou must not for a moment leave Sítá, Ráma, and Lakshmana. How will the ten-headed one, an enemy blind with pride, cunning, all powerful, matchless in might, and near at hand, bear the insult offered to his sister born from the same womb, and the destruction of his people time after time? Alas! the children must indeed be carefully guarded. I too after performing my daily vows on the sea-shore will pray that an increase of prosperity may happen. [*Exit.*

JATÁYU (*rising up and imitating flight in the sky*).

I here, drinking as it were the sky the vastness of which is contracted by my speed furious as the destructive wind, am swiftly come from the Malaya hill to the cluster of trees that grow upon the mountain-home. Here is the mountain named Prasravana, the caverns of which re-echo with the mighty river Godávarí, which has neighbouring forests, spotless, and pleasant, and crowded with dense collections of trees, — the blackness of which is increased by the clouds that are ever raining, which lies in the centre of Janasthana; and this is Pańchavatí. (*Looking round.*) Ah! Ráma has been allured afar off by the spotted deer; Lakshmana too is going in that direction. Therefore the ten-headed one here, whose form, alas! is well known, has entered the cottage in the guise of an ascetic.

What rashness! That wicked one has placed the young bride in his chariot drawn by more than a thousand demon-headed asses, and is going somewhere. Rávana! Rávana! your birth is in the line of those who were keepers of the holy Veda in the times of deluge, lords of the worlds, and you were perfected in Vaidic vows, and you are the conqueror of him whose palace is the water, and a king proud by reason of your penance; how then has this wicked purpose arisen within you, a purpose blameworthy, and of evil act, and unbecoming your high birth? How is this, that through contempt he appears not to hearken? Ah, evil-minded one! outcast of the demons! stop, stop. Let the son of Cyení glut himself with thy members, while all thy entrails drip with blood issuing warm from the liver, spleen, and lungs, which are visible and quivering as they are dragged through the top of the skull of thy head, which is split in two by my beak; while thy bones rattle, and are broken with my claws which pierce as a very sharp saw; and the blood-vessels of thy neck are broken into pieces.

[*Exit.*

END OF VISHKAMBHAKA.

Enter LAKSHMANA.

Ah, Princess! where art thou? Alas! the noble Ráma feels the sad change of his state which Márícha has caused. He, like anger embodied, or like a moving fire of grief, hardly bears the distraction of his body by flames of heart-ache. For with the fire of his anger furious and far-spread, by reason of his sorrow, which, though moderated by his firmness, yet throbs within, and is made known by the knitting of the deep frowns of his bending brows, he assumes the colour of a cloud charged with thunderbolts indicated by its lightnings, like the treasure of waters * encircled by ascending smoke and having the secret fire flashing in its midst.

Enter RÁMA.

RÁMA.

The outrage painfully rankles in my heart like a pointed thunderbolt. My mind shrinks with shame and seems to sink in the terrible and blinding darkness. The sorrow caused by the death of our dear friend burns me, and there is no help; but here the pity I feel for poor Sítá pierces my vitals.

LAKSHMANA.

Prince! Prince! Such as thou whose deeds are superhuman despair not in the midst of difficulties.

RÁMA.

Child! the deeds of Ráma are indeed superhuman.† Those ancient kings of men, by whom the worlds were protected and freed from fear, of great splendour, bearing the banners of the family of the sun, have been insulted; and that good Jatáyu who lived even in the ends of the ages of the world, has been sent to heaven. Truly, when I allowed my wife to be carried off in the

* The ocean.

† This is said in irony.

forest, I committed an act which was not committed by men in the world. Alas! Dear Káçyapa, king of birds! when again will be the birth of one like thee, so great, so holy, and so good?

LAKSHMANA.

Methinks I see that last state of the dear Jatáyu. "That Sítá, whom thou, long-lived Prince, dost seek like a healing plant in every forest, she and my life have both been taken away by Rávana." After speaking these words, Jatáyu ascended to the world of heroes.

RÁMA.

Brother! brother! The mention of these stories indeed pierces the depths of my heart.

LAKSHMANA.

And therefore we will by all means be quit of the debt of enmity towards that evil-minded one.

RÁMA.

True, but what can be done, that will be equal to the wanton infliction of so great an insult? Even aforetime, my mind was bent upon the destruction of the demons, since they deserve to be slain for many reasons. But when only that is accomplished, how can I get rest? The one supreme duty of our race is their destruction. Still, my child, the anger which is fierce and compressed into a ball, and the course of which is silent, which points inward, seeming to drink again and again and suddenly flaming upwards, issuing forth as it were by its flames, and not possessing any other object to consume, burns me, as the hidden fire burns the ocean. Deliver me from it.

LAKSHMANA.

These forests, in which the herds of various deer are greatly terrified, wherein the mountain caverns are frightful, and tenanted by races of beasts fierce and wild, face the southern quarter: therefore we will go in these very paths.

RÁMA.

Surely these divisions of Janasthána were not before seen.

LAKSHMANA.

Yes. Then at all events when we set out from the hermitage of Panchavatí, after committing to the flames the dear Áruni, the king of vultures; but now the boundaries of Janasthána are far distant. And since these woods in front excite fear, assuredly this is a part of the Dandaká forest, west of Janasthána, and named Kuńjaván, and occupied by the headless demon Danu.

RÁMA.

I must indeed see that cruel-minded frog of the forest.

(*A voice behind the scenes.*)

Who is here? Oh! help, help a woman dragged in the forest by this wicked headless demon. For I am a sylph, named Cramaná, performing penance, and an inhabitant of the hermitage of Matanga; and am come in search of Ráma.

RÁMA.

Dear Lakshmana! go, go.

LAKSHMANA.

I am gone. [*Exit.*

RÁMA.

Darling, where art thou? Send forth thy sweet voice. Those who are oppressed, as I am, cannot easily obtain even the joy of lamentation. Let Paulastya go blameless, but let censure fall upon me. Now that our enmity has increased, manifold mischief has been wrought by him.

Enter LAKSHMANA *and* CRAMANÁ.

LAKSHMANA.

That face and body, with its distorted form of the long-armed demon, whose bushy beard was wet with blood, pouring from the mass of beasts cut up by his cruel saw-like teeth, was not seen by my noble brother, though anxious to behold demons.

Noble Cramaná! here is the Prince!

CRAMANÁ.

Victory, victory to the bright one!

RÁMA.

What then is your object in seeking me?

CRAMANÁ.

Thou hast heard of Vibhíshana, the younger brother of Rávana.

RÁMA.

Who has not heard of him?

CRAMANÁ.

When through fate Khara, Dúshana, and the rest were slain, then at length from some cause or other he started from his kinsmen, and through the friendship of Sugríva, now dwells on Rishya-múka. Here is a letter delivered by his own hand.

[*With this she delivers the letter.*

LAKSHMANA (*taking it and reading*).

Greeting! Vibhíshana pays homage to the divine Ráma, and requests leave to inform him: "We, who have lost our good fortune, have but two last alternatives, either an increase of holiness, or your majesty the defender of holiness."

RÁMA.

Say then, my dear brother, what answer must be sent to the great king Vibhíshana, our dear friend, the ruler of Lanká, highly honoured, who thus speaks.

LAKSHMANA.

When my noble brother calls him "the ruler of Lanká, our dear friend," what answer is there left?

RÁMA.

Be it as the son of Sumitrá says.

CRAMANÁ.

We are favoured.

LAKSHMANA.

Noble Cramaná! say, hast thou any tidings of the Princess from thy intercourse with Vibhíshana?

CRAMANÁ.

At present none; but when she was carried off by that evil-minded and vilest of demons, her upper garment, marked with the name of Anasúyá, fell and was picked up by them.

RÁMA.

Ah, darling! dear friend of my abode in the great forest, daughter of the king of Videha.

[*Thus speaking he tries to conceal his grief.*

LAKSHMANA.

Noble one! by whom and for what purpose was it picked up?

CRAMANÁ.

On Rishyamúka by Sugríva, Vibhíshana, Hanúman, and others.

RÁMA.

Those high-minded beings, who freely confer favours upon me, and whose greatness is worthy of the world's respect, must be seen, as must also that token, Sítá's garment which fell; therefore, we will go towards Rishyamúka.

CRAMANÁ.

This way then, my lord.

[*With these words she walks round.*

LAKSHMANA.

The name "Hanuman," is the title of a great warrior; and stories of marvellous deeds, by which gods and demons were perplexed, are told of that great one immediately after his birth. Besides, it is well known, whatever might belongs to Indra who wields the thunderbolt, or whatever greatness belongs to the wind-god, and to the great armed Válí, the same belongs to the hero Hanuman.

CRAMANÁ.

True, such is the son of Añjaná, Hanuman by name, born of the wife of Kesarí, the aged chieftain of the powerful monkeys, high in honour, inhabitant of the golden mountain; but the father that begot him is the divine air. What then can we say of Hanuman alone? countless hundreds of thousands of those monkeys who drink with the hollow of their hands the water of the ocean like the juice of the cocoa-nut, and the cause of whose leaping on the mountains is this forest of fig-trees, and who are able to destroy the world with their might like the tree their dwelling-place, bow down to the son of the king of gods.

RÁMA.

Lady! towards the south there is a very large mass of fire. What is it?

CRAMANÁ.

'Tis the funeral pile of that long-armed demon made by the Prince Lakshmana.

RÁMA.

Well done!

LAKSHMANA.

Look, look! Noble Ráma! Streams of blood large with fulness boil up, exciting wonder; and the bones from the shrinking of the skin and flesh start out with hideous crackling; and foaming waves rise upwards from the destruction of the marrow. A wonder! a wonder! some divine being comes forth from this burying-place.

Enter a DEMIGOD, DANU.

DANU.

May the divine Ráma be victorious! I, who am the son of Crí, by name Danu, brought by a curse to the state of a demon and reduced to a headless trunk by the weapons of Indra, am purified by meeting with your majesty.

RÁMA.

We are pleased.

DANU.

I, employed by Mályaván, marred the forest in order to effect your ruin. But away with the recollection of the misery of that time; now that through your power my natural splendour increases, a certain hidden thing appears to me; and that for your information I will declare to you, who have rendered me great assistance. Válí at the urgent request of Mályaván is employed in your destruction, and he too adheres closely to his friendship with Rávana.

RÁMA.

This, and this only, is the way with those of noble

conduct. Such a friend assumes not a neutral state in time of action. My mind too is filled with longing towards that great hero.

OTHERS.

Where save in Ráma would these words be found?

RÁMA.

Good! the duty of a good friend has now been performed. Joy to thee, happy one, in thine own world!

DANU.

As your majesty commands. [*Exit.*

LAKSHMANA.

Lady! what is the bond of friendship between Válí and Rávana?

CRAMANÁ.

When the son of Indra placed under his armpit the ten-headed one who was prepared to wage a war of hands, and was proud because he had shaken the mountain Kailása, and conquered the three worlds; and after performing at twilight his wonted rites in the seven oceans, let him go; on that occasion he granted friendship to him whom he had released, and who humbly craved it.

LAKSHMANA.

Evil-minded one! disgrace to the race of Paulastya! Such is thy excess of valour, thou bane of Kshatriyas.

RÁMA.

The world of living beings is strange, in that it ever possesses one superior above another.

LAKSHMANA.

Lady! what is the name of this pleasant mountain in front of thee?

CRAMANÁ.

This is no mountain; but a heap of bones of Dundubhi, the mighty chief of Daityas, like a mound of the hero Válí's fame.

LAKSHMANA.

These paths are blocked up, therefore let us avoid them.

RÁMA.

Nay, come! [*He kicks the heap with his foot.*

CRAMANÁ.

A marvel! Ráma here by the movement of his great toe drives entirely hence that skeleton, which resembled a grey cloud out of season, and blocked our path,—the skeleton of Dundubhi, the enemy of the gods, who occupied the mountain,—which the chief of monkeys, the son of Indra, squeezing by the efforts of his stalwart arms, cast out.

LAKSHMANA.

The land of the mountain and forest of great beauty, blue, grand, and calm, draws near.

CRAMANÁ.

These indeed are the lands in the neighbourhood of Rishyamúka, and the lake Pampá; and in front is also the hermitage-ground of Matanga, where in the absence of the saint the divino fire-god burns even now, with its fuel and holy grass spread around, and its collections of special sacrificial vessels, and Soma cups placed near.

RÁMA.

Excellence of penance is attended by prosperity which surpasses thought.

ÇRAMANÁ.

Look, look! my lord! Here the mountain torrents flow with their waters, clear, and cold, and fragrant with the flowers that fall from the canes filled with loving birds; and their broad currents resound with the dashing of the water against the creeper-houses of the rose-apple, black with the ripening of its abundant fruit. Again, here the cries of the young boars that tenant the mountain caves attain an increase magnified by the re-echoes; and the perfume of the sap from the knots of the Sallakí trees, which are broken and scattered by the elephants, spreads around,—cool, aromatic, and fragrant.

LAKSHMANA.

How is it that my noble brother suddenly stands still, imitating the movement of a hero with his body leaning upon his bow, and surveying with his eye, from which floods of tears fall, the forests of Kadamba trees which are shaken by the strong east wind?

ÇRAMANÁ.

Child! dost thou not see? There stand the Kadamba trees with their buds now closed, though their opening is near at hand; and a wild dance is performed by the peacocks, whose notes are very sweet; and the new cloud dark as the Tápiñcha blossom when full grown, and opening at the top, spreads over the peak of the mountain.

LAKSHMANA (*speaking to himself*).

Perhaps my noble brother here is overcome by some other emotion.

(*A voice behind the scenes.*)

Grandfather return! At thy command the slaughter of a good man, although improper, shall be made. Assuredly thou dost deserve my respect; for he, who is the superior of a friend, is indeed a superior.

LAKSHMANA.

Lady! who comes here?

CRAMANÁ.

My Lord! see, see! The son of Indra,—wearing a beautiful necklace of golden lotuses, given by Indra, and with his yellow body resembling a large cloud charged with lightning and tinged with the twilight; and possessing the splendour of a mountain marked with red earth on its peaks, which has been rent by upheavings,—from his speed leaves a track in the sky like an inner line of the parting of the hair.

LAKSHMANA.

Brother, brother! the son of Indra is come, a friend who kindly affords a meeting of warriors.

RÁMA (*speaking to himself*).

He is a great hero.

Enter VÁLÍ.

VÁLÍ.

I can cut the post of Brahma, so that the stream of the seventh ocean will sparkle with ripples in the water-basin Lokáloka, and the three worlds of former ages will fall to pieces, and the root the lower world will be entirely dug out, and the cluster-like sun and moon will be scattered abroad, and the countless stars like to flowers, will fall down: but in this action I feel sharp pain. Men who engage in an improper act like this are hurled into a huge unseemly pit. Since this Mályaván by reminding me of my friendship with Rávana has employed me in the destruction of the noble Ráma, the banner of the Raghu race. Oh, the demon! from early morn he has followed me, and after inducing me to set out from Kishkindhá he has now returned. Alas! alas! when a guest, who was pure from his natural uprightness, holy-minded, and worthy of the respect of the worlds, and deceived by guileful enemies through their villany, came even to my own house, towards him proper treatment was not shown; a kind word was not spoken, even by my tongue. Alas! why did I, wicked one that I am, make an attempt to kill him as if he were a foe? And now the spies bring this report. Vibhíshana, without telling even Sugríva, has dispatched Cramaná to Ráma; and the son of Dacaratha, who has promised him the sovereignty of Lanká, is staying in the neighbourhood of this hermitage of Matanga. Be it so, I will descend. (*He imitates a descent.*) Ho! who is there? I am come to see the pleasant one, who vanquished

Paracuráma, who is pleasing by reason of his truth and holiness, a treasure-house of virtues. When he has been seen, the eye has fulfilled its object; and there arises an agreeable tickling as from the itch of pride.

RÁMA.

Dear son of Sumitrâ! tell the fortunate one that I stand here.

LAKSHMANA (*approaching*).

Here stands the Prince, let the fortunate one approach.

VÁLÍ.

And art thou the famed Lakshmana?

LAKSHMANA.

I am. [*Both approach.*

VÁLÍ (*speaking to himself*).

This is that Ráma winning by his noble conduct, a hero matchless in holiness, the best of men, peerless, who surpasses only his own former deeds by other later deeds of great wonder.* (*Aloud.*) Ráma! to my joy and surprise, or to my sorrow, I look upon thee. But now, how can my eye be satisfied in beholding thee? I am not meet for the pleasure of thy embrace. Of what use therefore is idle talking? Let the bow be bent in that hand of thine, which is famous for the humbling of Jámadagnya.

RÁMA.

'Tis by good fortune that thou art this day seen; and

* *i.e.*, None but his own former achievements are worthy to be put in comparison.

this that thou sayest is indeed proper. But how can Ráma wear a weapon against you who are without weapons?

VÁLÍ (*smiling*).

Great warrior! why dost thou pity us who need not thy pity? We are surely known in the worlds by our noble conduct; what then can be said in words? Get ready. Truth belongs to your highness: your highness is a true man. We, for the most part are such, that our conquest is not thwarted by means of weapons; but if you wish me to take up one, then those mountains, by which the monkeys are furnished with weapons, breathe success. From this place, therefore, let us descend to level ground.

LAKSHMANA.

Noble brother! it is as the fortunate one says; the laws of war are determined by the customs of each respective class.

VÁLÍ *and* RÁMA (*speaking of each other*).

Assuredly the great festival of a heroic meeting with thee would be praiseworthy; but now, since thou hast passed thy time, the earth will be without a hero.

[*They walk round and leave the stage.*

LAKSHMANA.

How was it that as soon as the bow twanged the son of Indra was angry? For, with a roar terrible as a thundering cloud, ceaseless, and shrill, and loud, he hisses within. And with all the quarters of the world entering into his mouth, that is widely opened in a yawn, and which is like a Gunja-seed in colour; and with his banner-like tail, yellow as the lightning, spread out and standing high with erection from excitement, he swells out and shakes his expanded body with pride, covering the canopy of the sky.

(*A voice behind the scenes.*)

Vibhíshana! Vibhíshana! this is like the cry of the noble Válí. Surely 'tis his and none other; for it is fierce as the thunder of a new cloud. Whence can be this frightful twang of the bow-string? Is it the Pináka bow made use of by Civa?

LAKSHMANA.

Lady, who is this?

CRAMANÁ.

He is Sugríva, the friend of Vibhíshana, and he follows the war with jealousy and anger; and all the chieftains are assembling from the mountain caverns.

LAKSHMANA.

Then I too must now string my bow.

CRAMANÁ.

That arrow has now rested in the quiver of Ráma, after piercing the body of Váli, the skull of Dundubhi, the seven palm-trees, the mountain, and the earth's surface.

(*A voice behind the scenes.*)

Let Vibhíshana and Sugríva take an oath, at my death, to be calm. Oh, brave monkeys! be tranquil. If I am, as of old, your chieftain to-day, this is the prayer I make, having met with the highly honourable death of a warrior from Ráma. Let* the son of the sun here be to you as I am, and let the child Angada be to you as he is.

LAKSHMANA.

The son of Indra here,—beheld by his generals, while they conceal their grief which is intolerable, and plainly visible in the assembly, where they are released from their duty as warriors by the constraining behest given to his followers, beheld too by my noble brother with tears of affection; while the safety of his body is inquired after by Vibhíshana, full of sorrow and held back by the oath taken at his hour of death; while the thrill of pain from the cruel stroke which pierced his vitals is with great effort suppressed; and while under the disguise of an embrace he clasps firmly the neck of Sugríva, and hangs around it the string of the necklace of golden lotuses taken from his own neck, even in this state shines with the glory of a warrior.

Enter SUGRÍVA, VIBHÍSHANA, VÁLÍ, *and* RÁMA.

RÁMA.

The change that wrought the death of such as these whose conduct, fame, prowess, and birth is rare, and glory pure, and strength vast as a great mountain, is painful indeed. Alas! death, all-injuring and cruel, works mischief.

VÁLÍ.

Dear Vibhíshana! see, see! the necklace-band of

* Válí here appoints his successors. Sugríva is to take Válí's place, and Angada to take Sugríva's place.

a thousand lotuses shines well on the chest of the child Sugríva.

SUGRÍVA *and* VIBHÍSHANA (*aside*).

What is this change wrought by the Creator, cruel and terrible as the thunderbolt, when it falls suddenly and without rain? How are we, bound as we are by oath, to disobey our chief? and how are we to sit quiet?

VÁLÍ.

Rámabhadra! Rámabhadra!

RÁMA.

Noble one! I am here.

VALÍ.

I have now paid with my life the debt due to that friendship, which through destiny I formed with a man whose friendship I desired not; and that other duty, which is seemly towards the good, and towards thee, a storehouse of virtues,—that also I have discharged to the utmost of my power at the close of my life.

[RÁMA *stands with sorrow, shame, and humility.*

SUGRÍVA *and* VIBHÍSHANA (*aside*).

Noble Cramaná, how is it that this change of destiny comes from the divine Ráma who is like a pool of nectar?

CRAMANÁ.

'Tis through Mályaván indeed.

[*She whispers in the ears of both.*

VÁLÍ.

Dear Sugríva.

[*Sugríva tries to suppress his tears.*

VÁLÍ.

Truly Sugríva has become hostile.

SUGRÍVA (*sorrowfully*).

My noble brother! be gracious. Give me your commands.

VÁLÍ.

Dear Sugríva! tell me what am I to thee?

SUGRÍVA.

My teacher and lord.

VÁLÍ.

And what art thou to me.

SUGRÍVA.

Pupil and servant.

VÁLÍ.

Say, dear, what are our respective duties?

SUGRÍVA.

Yours to rule and mine to serve.

VÁLÍ (*taking him by the hand*).

Then I give thee to Ráma. Rámabhadra! do thou receive him.

RÁMA *and* SUGRÍVA.

Who does not highly respect the word of our honoured master?

VIBHÍSHANA.

Brief words on a great subject, yet pure and full of duty.

VÁLÍ.

Dear Sugríva! what is the law of friendship that thou who hast studied all the laws of duty hast learned from Jámbaván, thy teacher, the son of the supreme.

SUGRÍVA.

Good conduct maintained even at the cost of life, freedom from wrong-doing, avoidance of guile, and pleasant actions, as if to one's self,—this is the great vow of friendship.

VÁLÍ.

Rámabhadra, this only is the doctrine thou too hast received from the holy Vasishtha, the family priest to the race of the sun.

RÁMA.

Noble one, it is.

VÁLÍ.

Then you must practise through life this law of friendship to each other; and at my request let an oath be taken witnessed by the fire: the moment must not pass. Here just at hand is the sacrificial fire of Matanga.

RÁMA *and* SUGRÍVA (*taking each other's hand*).

In the holy sacrificial fire of Matanga our friendship is formed: let my heart be thine, and thy heart mine.

VÁLÍ.

Rámabhadra! here too is the dear Vibhíshana, to whom

thou didst promise the sovereignty of Lanká in the presence of Cramaná.

VIBHÍSHANA (*with shame and suspicion*).

How am I found out?

CRAMANÁ *and* LAKSHMANA.

Ah! the power of seeing through spies!

RÁMA.

Very true.

VIBHÍSHANA.

Then I had the favour of your majesty.

[*He bows.*

SUGRÍVA.

I am surprised when I think that the message of Cramaná, though untold even to me, has been successful.

RÁMA.

My dear friends, great Kings Sugríva and Vibhíshana, this is now your Saumitri.

LAKSHMANA.

Princes! I Lakshmana greet you.

Both.

Come here, dear one!

[*They embrace him.*

CRAMANÁ.

That reception is grand and affectionate.

VÁLÍ.

Child Vibhíshana! away now with anxiety about thy

affairs. This matter must thus end, for Rávana is no more; this is made known by my story. Though our grandfather has equal affection for his children, still it is his special duty to guard the interests of Rávana, seeing that he lives at his table, and to declare in full the union of Vibhíshana with his friend. The great alone know the bold attempts of such as he, whose nature is unfathomable. My life ebbs away, lead me therefore to the place where is the vault of death.

Níla and you others, alas! oh warrior! alas! son of Indra! thou whose might was immovable as the mountain Mandara. A warrior peerless in the world, the clasp of whose stalwart arms was terrible and fierce in the slaughter of the haughty Dundubhi, thou art gone! Alas! we are slain!

[*Thus speaking and supported by them weeping he walks round.*

VÁLÍ.

Oh! noble-minded and excellent monkeys, that the sovereignty here belongs to Sugríva and Angada is owing to your good nature; and from your attachment to me, indeed, it must not be slighted, and this will be in keeping with your greatness. Already the war between Ráma and Rávana is at hand to test your friendship, 'tis about this I implore you. But cease; what are we to you in valour? Again, those destructions of the two pairs of sky-guarding elephants bereft of their ears, and those leaps into the lower world through the chasms of the ocean which opens beneath the blows of your tail, and that conduct which is well becoming your monkey-prowess, and affection, and greatness, and your arms by which enemies are crushed, must not escape your minds.

[*Exeunt omnes.*

END OF THE FIFTH ACT.

ACT VI.

Enter MÁLYAVÁN *downcast.*

MÁLYAVÁN (*thoughtfully*).

Ah! the buds of the tree of the demon-king's bad policy seem scattered all around. Its seed was the request for the daughter of the king of Videha; its sprout the journey of his sister; the guileful act of Márícha to deceive those two the sapling; the rape of her who is not born of a woman the collection of branches; the death of the lord of the treasure and the departure of his younger brother and his friendship with those two are clearly its buds. And very soon indeed, I think, this tree will bear fruit; since the mind of the aged sees that which has not yet happened. (*Sighing.*) Alas! the perverseness of fortune! In this calamity, whatever remedy I applied by the power of counsel, each one came to naught of itself like the act of an idle man. (*With pain.*) The office of minister tends to great sorrow. Whatsoever the haughty desire with self-will and unrestrainedly, in each case a remedy must be devised, even though destiny is adverse.

Alas! the all-surpassing deeds of the evil-minded warrior-boy! What did he not achieve, when he curbed by his arrows the ruler of monkeys, the fire of whose courage is so great? (*After reflecting.*) And it was reported by the spy who had returned from Kishkindhá, that the powerful monkeys repaired to every quarter to search out Sítá.

(*A voice behind the scenes.*)

Fire whirling with red circles of more than seven flames having rapidly spread, unperceived by the warriors, in the golden houses heated beyond measure,—fire so great that a fear of the end of the world fills the minds of the warlike demons who are running away half-burnt, breaking out on all sides devours Lanká, with the mountain Trikúta as far as the ocean.

Enter TRIJATÁ *in great alarm, throwing aside the curtain.*

TRIJATÁ.

Save, save me! good grandfather!

[*She falls beating her breast.*

MÁLYAVÁN.

Child! away with this fright. What means this great cry that is raised?

TRIJATÁ (*rising up*).

Good grandfather! what can I say, unhappy one that I am? Some wicked monkey here, after setting fire to the whole city in a moment, drove out the world of countless demons the same instant like deer in their flight; and when attacked even by the Prince Aksha, practised upon him the play of death, and suddenly went out.

MÁLYAVÁN (*painfully*).

What! Is the city burned, and the Prince Aksha slain? Can it be a monkey indeed? (*Remembering.*) It was reported by the spy that Hanúman had gone to the south. Alas! was the fierce valour of the king of Lańká quenched by Hanúman, while he burned his capital Lańká as one burns cotton?

Child! did he obtain any tidings of Sítá?

TRIJATÁ.

Good grandfather! this much I know, that even before this a very small monkey was seen taking counsel with her, and she unfastened and gave into his hand her hair-adornment, saying, "It is a token."

MÁLYAVÁN.

What has not been done? (*With fear.*) That very small monkey alone accomplished so much. More than hundreds of millions of such are now heard of in the monkey-tribe, protected by the strength of the arm of Sugríva.

TRIJATÁ (*thoughtfully*).

How is it, that Sítá, being a mortal, so mild in appearance, so gentle in conduct, became a demon even to us who are demons?

MÁLYAVÁN.

Child! it is nevertheless correct. 'Tis the brightness

of chastity to her husband that is thus declared, calm, and glorious. (*After thinking.*) And yet what has that unhappy one to do with it?

This is but the evil consequence of his bad actions flaming forth spontaneously.

TRIJATÁ.

Grandfather! at first we demons had our abode merely on parts of the various mountains that stand in the neighbourhood of the Dandaká forest, while our pleasure grounds were over the whole of Jambudvípa; but now our abode even in this city is impossible. What can be done? What remedy can we devise?

MÁLYAVÁN.

Child! why art thou thus afraid? See, here is the fortress Chitrakúta, and above it is the city with its seven walls like the seven elements of the body; and this its trench, which is hard to cross and without boundary, is the ocean whose waves touch the sky. (*Reflecting.*) And yet what of this? We must look only to the stalwart arms of the demon-king, which are ready to subdue the proud enemy, as a great sacrifice. (*Exhibiting a throbbing of his left eye, painfully.*) What can our destiny be in connection with these words? Its sad change is unbearable. Child! how much is yet left of the period of Prince Kumbhakarna's sleep?

TRIJATÁ.

Grandfather! on this very day of the dark fortnight, the fourth month is completed.

MÁLYAVÁN.

What! is the time of his awaking so very distant even now? (*Remembering.*) But, when I think over it, alas! only the young boy is far-seeing, whose habit of acting without thought produces good results; and when I reflect again and again, I look forward only to him as the source of the continuance of our race.

TRIJATÁ (*trembling*).

My grandfather! alas! alas! may the evil be destroyed and the bad omen averted.

MÁLYAVÁN.

What is it?

TRIJATÁ.

These words of policy that my grandfather has uttered have only ended in another evil omen.

MÁLYAVÁN.

Child! it was not because I wished it that I spake this. But thus it will terminate. For he falls not in any place except where something great is to result, and he has not a thought of evil, being pure by his birth like this sun, which leaving the mountain where it sets revolves in the boundless sky, and is followed by the light of day. Therefore in the remedies against this, it is only left for us to wake up our sleeping mind. Enough of this. Child! knowest thou in what matter our chief Rávana is occupied?

TRIJATÁ.

Grandfather! our king has now ascended the tower

called all-fortunate, and stands looking at the grove of Acoka-trees, where she who is a night of destruction to the race of demons dwells; besides, as I was coming here, I heard these tidings, that the queen too, grieved at heart upon hearing the account about our city, was gone thither to inform him of his danger.

MÁLYAVÁN.

Child! the Queen Mandodarí, whose mind is anxious to inform him, is superior, woman as she is; but not so the king, who though informed rouses not himself. Therefore come, let us go within, and consider what our spies must do.

[*Exeunt.*

END OF THE VISHKAMBHAKA.

Enter RÁVANA (*full of longing*).

RÁVANA (*beholding* SITÁ).

If her face be here, what need is there of the moon? If her eyes with rolling glances, what need of clusters of lotuses? If her brows arched like waves, what need of the bow of the self-born one? If her well-pressed hair, what need of lines of clouds? If this her body, what need of the goddess of beauty?

(*With pleasure arising from memory.*) Oh! now that I am in the enjoyment of that pearl of women, that came forth from the all-nourishing earth when pierced by the mouth of the plough, my wish has borne fruit after a long time. (*Reflecting.*) This surely is the trust of propitious destiny. (*Proudly.*) But what is this destiny? If I should crush the universe, and then from this division of the world raise up another, and give Brahmá his place of authority; and, after making his peerless and brilliant glory, and his fame into a sun aud moon, should then take much repose, there would be no blame of idleness. (*With compassion.*) But what anger can there be towards those who deserve my pity?

Enter MANDODARÍ *and a* HANDMAID.

HANDMAID.

Here, lady! this is the entrance to the way of the silver staircase, therefore let my lady ascend.

MANDODARÍ (*beholding* RÁVANA).

How is it that the great king Rávana remains here? (*Looking intently.*) Why does he look towards the grove of Acoka-trees? (*With pain.*) How comes it that when such an attack is made by an ally of the enemy, the great king Rávana seems indifferent to his duty as a king? (*Approaching near.*) May the great ten-headed king be victorious!

RÁVANA (*showing a suppression of his emotions*).

What! is it Mandodarí?

[*Thus speaking, he makes her sit down at his side.*

MANDODARÍ (*obeying*).

Oh, great king! what thinkest thou about this matter?

RÁVANA.

What matter?

MANDODARÍ.

The attack made by the enemy's ally.

RÁVANA (*with a loud laugh*).

What! that there is an enemy, that he has an ally, and that he has made an attack—this that my queen has heard is a thing unheard of. I with my two arms at once resisted the tusks of the wild sky-guarding elephants on the field of battle; and with my four hands opposed by main force even the lords of the celestial quarters, aforetime unvanquished; and the skin of my chest is scarred by the fall of weapons, the flaming thunder-bolt, and others: but still I am rivalled, and have an enemy. This that is spoken is some unheard of madness.

Be it so; still, I should like to hear, O Queen, who he is.

MANDODARÍ.

'Tis reported to be Ráma the son of Dacaratha, accompanied by his younger brother; and his general is Sugríva, who is followed by hosts of monkeys of all sorts.

RÁVANA.

What! the ascetic and his younger brother. What of that ill-fated one? What will he do by their means?

MANDODARÍ.

It is the host that is dreaded, O great king. Besides, after he had encamped his army on the shore of the ocean, he summoned the ocean-god; and, when he did not come forth from his abode, then he (*here the queen changes from Prákrit to Sanskrit*) shot an arrow a little within the cavity of the ocean, by the might of which in half a moment the whole water, revolving again and again with the motion of a wheel, became crimson with boiling; and its shoals of sea-monsters began to faint, and its swarms of tortoises suddenly to burst asunder, and its countless mermen to swoon; while a strange sound rang out, and its shells and pearls were plainly seen.

RÁVANA (*with contempt*).

What then?

MANDODARÍ.

Then, O great king, the ocean-god, with his body covered with numbers of sharp arrows, the ends only of which were visible, came forth from the water; and honouring him by falling at his feet, pointed out the way; and thus friendship was formed with that bold one. So it is reported.

RÁVANA (*with laughter*).

Be it so, it is reported. What sort of way is it, O queen?

MANDODARÍ.

O great king! a causeway is made by means of mountains brought by thousands of monkeys.

RÁVANA.

Queen! thou hast been deceived by some one. The great depth of this lord-of-waters is indeed unknown; surely not even a corner of his belly would be filled by all the mountains that are in Jambudvípa, or the other islands.

Beside, when the queen called him bold, she had almost forgotten my boldness; but my witness is Civa, to whom water for the feet was offered in streams of my blood, fresh, and pouring largely from the veins of my necks which kept growing up: whose feet too were honoured with my heads in place of lotuses, the beauty of which shone in smiles, which had tears of joy like abundant honey.

MANDODARÍ.

Know, O great king, that the structure of the bank is somewhat strange; for at the touch of the hand of a certain monkey those rocks stand up on the water.

RÁVANA (*shaking his head*).

To fancy "that rocks swim," is that incurable ignorance of women. Queen, what need of more words? The poet of sacred lore knows my learning, the husband of Cachí my command, the thunderbolt my strength, these three worlds my fame, the mountain Kailása my power. What more? Oh! the god of the keen-edged axe, whose feet were bathed in my streaming blood instead of water, knows my daring also.

[*Behind the scenes a loud confused cry.*

MANDODARÍ.

O great king! help! help!

[*With these words she looks at him with fear.*

RÁVANA.

O queen! away with thy fear.

(*Again a voice behind the scenes*).

O troops of demons that guard the gates of Lanká! Give up quickly your tall and heavy gates, throw down the bolts heavy as rocks; then bring forth all your arms, and think of your families; keep the lives of your children and young women free of harm, and have regard for your stores of grain. Rámabhadra accompanied by his younger brother, and surrounded by monkeys headed by Sugríva, is come.

The CHAMBERMAID *half enters from behind the scenes.*

CHAMBERMAID.

Here on the threshold of the door stands the General Prahasta desirous of informing your majesty.

RÁVANA.

What! the General Prahasta? Let him enter.

CHAMBERMAID.

As your majesty commands. [*Exit.*

Enter PRAHASTA.

PRAHASTA.

Oh! the all-powerful deeds of the stripling of a man. For he crossed like a mere cow's track the lord of waters (ocean), which was terrible and rough, with a line of huge breakers on all sides; and approaching slowly with his eyes fixed upon Lanká encamped his army on the rugged top of the mountain Suvelá, and then surrounded by certain powerful monkeys occupies in person the outskirts of the city. (*Looking in front.*) What! is this the king of Lanká?

RÁVANA.

My good general! what is the cause of this loud noise?

PRAHASTA (*speaking to himself*).

What! is the king still in ignorance? Let it be, I will inform him of the state of affairs. (*Aloud.*) The city has been carefully secured, the gates are closed, and a defence is maintained on all sides by the trusty and loyal demons.

RÁVANA.

What is this?

PRAHASTA (*to himself*).

How is it that he is in the very same state? Let it be. (*Aloud.*) Sire, king of Lanká! thy city is blockaded by a mere stripling of a man who is accompanied by his younger brother, so that stores of grain, and the like, are hard to be got.

Enter the CHAMBERMAID.

CHAMBERMAID.

Sire! Here is a monkey who says that he is the ambassador of Ráma, and waits on the threshold.

RÁVANA (*with contempt*).

A monkey! Let him enter.

CHAMBERMAID.

As your highness commands. [*Exit.*

Enter with ANGADA. (*To Angada.*)

Here is the king! Approach.

ANGADA (*approaching*).

May the king of Lanká, the follower of the supreme one, be victorious!

RÁVANA.

You are a follower of Sugríva.

ANGADA.

Not so.

RÁVANA.

Whose then?

ANGADA.

O king of Lanká, listen who I am, and on what account I am come. I am an ambassador by the command of Ráma, who is like a terrible forest-fire to the armies of proud demons; and I am come to instruct thee in his words. Give up Sítá, and pay homage to the feet of Saumitri, accompanied by thy sons, kinsmen, friends, and females; otherwise, difficult as thou art to be vanquished, thou wilt be punished by his arrows.

RÁVANA (*laughing*).

Even the monkey is talkative. What should I say?

ANGADA.

I am of little account; but do thou finally determine. Shall thy heads this day be bowed down and touch the nails of his lotus-like feet, or the mouths of his sharp arrows? Say, which wilt thou of these two?

RÁVANA (*angrily*).

Who is here? Let him purify the mouth of this vain speaker.

PRAHASTA.

Sire! he is an ambassador. Is anger then proper?

RÁVANA.

To amend his mouth indeed would be an answer to the ascetic.

ANGADA (*gesticulating a thrill of excitement with bristling hair*).

Thinkest thou I would return without giving, as an offering to the quarters of heaven, thy heads which droop as the collar-bone is crushed by the bold attack of my claws piercing and rugged as a sharp saw, one claw to each head, if I were not dependent upon the will of another in that I am the ambassador of the chief of the Raghus?

[*He then jumps up and departs.*

RÁVANA (*watching*).

Ah! the agility easy to his race and beyond prevention!

PRAHASTA.

Sire! my heart longs to receive the line of letters containing your command.

RÁVANA.

What! Need any command be asked in this case? Let the bolts on all hands be broken, and let the battle be commenced on all sides by the demons, who are proud by reason of their strength famous in all worlds, and who are able to thrust back foes; and repelling the destructive weapons of the enemy, let their arms be broken in pieces; and let the monkeys who pride in their leaps and idle jumps be stricken down again and again.

(*Behind the scenes a loud cry; all listen with fear. Again a cry is heard behind the scenes*).

The bravest of the demons are slain by the chiefs of the monkeys whose stature is terrible, and the terraces are everywhere strewed with slaughtered fiends; and here these in their desire to escape outside, blind with passion, have been slain in the midst in a moment; and the tall gates are broken in every quarter by the huge rocks hurled at them.

RÁVANA (*looking up and watching angrily*).

How is it that, from attachment to the ascetics, the gods too, headed by Indra, who know not themselves, and are filled with emnity towards me, arouse themselves to the battle? Therefore, O queen! go within; and I too, with some of my arms, will scatter to the quarters of heaven the wild and overgrown monkeys; and with my other powerful arms I will crush those two stripling ascetics, the actors in performing the play of war; and with the rest I will drag down those wicked gods, who have merely taken advantage of my neglect, which is trivial, but is reflected in their own minds; and casting aside mercy, I will fill my prison with them.

[*He walks fiercely round and leaves the stage.*

Enter in a chariot INDRA *with Attendants and his Charioteer* MÁTALI.

MÁTALI.

Sire, ruler of the sky! Since here, over Lanká, a shout resounds loudly from the demons running to and fro, powerful, and rushing about more than thousands in number;—a shout furious as the sweep of conflicting waves in the seven oceans, which roll greatly as in the time of the deluge; therefore, I infer that the commander of the night-stalkers is about to march forth to battle.

INDRA.

Charioteer! see, see! The leader of demons, seeing the attack to be very firm, has suddenly thrown open the gates in haste; and accompanied by his sons, brothers, servants, and thousands of demons, is gone forth from the city, causing all the inhabitants of the forest to fly apart. (*He gesticulates listening to the sound.*) Ah! who is this, that comes here, in haste from the quarter of Kuvera in an aerial car garlanded with a wreath of golden tinkling bells?

CHARIOTEER.

Sire! it is Chitraratha; upon whom your majesty alone conferred the great favour of installing him in the sovereignty over the kingdom of heavenly spirits.

Enter CHITRARATHA *in an aerial car.*

CHITRARATHA.

Success to the king of the gods!

INDRA.

King of the heavenly spirits! is thy mind fixed upon seeing the battle?

CHITRARATHA.

That is one reason; but there is another also.

INDRA.

What other?

CHITRARATHA.

The command of the king of Alaká.

INDRA.

What manner of command?

CHITRARATHA.

A certain sickness* difficult to be cured, which has increased from the day of my birth, or, perhaps, one that prevails over the three worlds; this is the day of its destruction by the will of destiny. Whether its termination will be happy or unhappy, that is what I have been sent to learn.

INDRA.

Such is the wish even of kinsmen.

CHITRARATHA.

What wonder! for those relatives are mutual enemies.

* *i.e.*, Rávana.

The craftiness, too, of him, whose actions are bad and whose wont is to carry off the car and other treasures is well known. Nay rather, the whole range of living creatures in the three worlds, pained by his arrogant and evil deeds watches anxiously for the victory of the son of Raghu from its love to him.

INDRA (*looking intently*).

King of heavenly spirits! Since here, from the top of the mountain Suvelá, the army of monkeys has suddenly risen up in disorder, causing the ends of the quarters of the sky to re-echo with their loud screams; therefore, I think the demons have now hurled their weapons.

CHITRARATHA.

King of gods! see, see! The ruler of the demons here standing in his car huge as a mountain-peak, a leader* of those whose minds know well the joy of war, deafens on all sides the hollow vault of the sky with the ceaseless screams of living creatures, redoubled by the echoes of the mountains in the ends of the quarters.

INDRA.

King of Gandharvas! the equipment which it becomes warriors to use is not evenly balanced in the case of these two. (*In haste.*) Charioteer; offer my war chariot to Rámabhadra. I too will ascend the aerial car driven by the king of Gandharvas.

[*He does so.*

* A better reading would be *preshtha* = very dear to.

CHARIOTEER.

As the king commands.

[*Exit.*

CHITRARATHA.

King of the gods! how are we to avoid this turmoil? For the battle is begun by the huge demons and monkeys, who have suddenly broken their ranks, and whose senses are stunned by blows of the fist, and dragging of hair, and the discharge of arms; so that the way is become difficult to pass through by reason of the streams of blood, that spring forth from the corpses shrunken in the painful crush of bodies together. Again, here on the ground of the battlefield is a heap, raised up by the huge and haughty bodies of rival heroes stricken down by the act of cleaving their stalwart arms, which are large and skilful in severing the heads and trunks of warriors;—a heap rugged, and resembling the mountain Chitrakúta, where reptile-soldiers lurk in thousands, terrified by the attack of the enemy.

INDRA.

King of aerial spirits! Here the heroes, with their bodies smeared all over with streams of blood running from countless wounds caused by the blows of arms, desist from the attack, and rest for half a moment on the borders of the battlefield; while the heat of the sun is screened by the shadow of the broad pinions of the vulture-kings which are speeding in their haste to devour the hearts covered with torrents of blood pouring from warriors pierced with darts. Here too the combatants, through whose thick skin now torn away the flesh is hacked, while the mass of entrails is plainly seen, and the large blood-vessels, bones, and sinews are cut to pieces, each one in the pride of his valour, eagerly receive on their chests in front the sword of a rival.

CHITRARATHA.

King of gods! The entrance of the chief of demons into the battle is unparallelled in its manner. For well worthy to be seen on the field of battle is on the left side Meghanáda surrounded by his hundred brothers, and on the other side Kumbhakarna, who is roused up and whose pride is overbearing among heroes; here the circle of the kinsmen of Kaikasí, exceeding great, stands in the rear; while he who is most impenetrable, like the Vindhya mountain, occupies the centre sitting in the front of his chariot.*

INDRA.

King of aerial spirits! Rámabhadra is indeed fearless, though he sees the enemy who is bold in his attack. But this is truly becoming; since those lofty mountains, exceeding great in strength, move not a bit, though the loud storm-wind blows in every quarter; and those oceans too, the extent of which is unknown, and the greatness of whose waters is seen in their vast depth, leave not their boundary.

CHITRARATHA.

King of the gods! see, see! The mighty chieftain of the Raghus has left with sorrow his younger brother

* Here Rávana is meant, though his name is not given.

who is bent down in respect, and whose fingers bright as a young shoot are engaged in stringing his bow for the destruction of Meghanáda, and selecting for his aim the king of demons, who is skilled in the battle, and who is accompanied by his younger brother, adorns again with his touch the bow-string. How will this succeed? Methinks it is a difficult matter; for the demon warriors, each one assailing him, conceal the scion of the race of the sun with showers of arrows in thousands, making on all sides a simultaneous attack. And yet what is difficult? Even these two, passing strong, whose authority and greatness none can fully declare, and the discharge of whose arrows is telling in its effect of breaking the weapons of the enemy, shine brightly on the field of battle. (*Looking all around.*) Ah! how is it that even these monkeys in the great combat of the enemy, declaring their respective names, five or six only in number worship the sole of the foot of Rámabhadra? For Sugríva is in the front of the chariot, and Angada here at the back, Jámbaván and the future king of Lanká on the two sides, five or six only. (*Reflecting.*) But Hanúman waits upon the younger descendant of Kakutstha. (*Excitedly.*) 'Tis well for two reasons that they only are attendants upon the lotus-like feet of Rámabhadra; since in their case loyalty to their master and courage declare their bodies to be unscathed; but in the case of the rest the attack made by the demons, and their own utter helplessness, is plainly seen.

INDRA.

King of aerial spirits! in the world of mortals compassion is a mere handful of powder, which can make subject all the senses; for the son of Sumitrá is not inferior in certain qualities, such as dexterity of hand; and the son of Rávana who excels in valour, and whose greatness is well known, is not inferior in strength; while thus their respective powers are evenly matched, a shower of arrows indeed keeps flying between Ráma and the chief of demons, but all the while their glances are filled with compassion.

CHITRARATHA.

King of the gods! this is very proper. Thus the high-minded feel the impulse of compassion. (*With great eagerness.*) Mark, O king! The night-stalkers, like lofty mountains, sorely wounded to their very vitals by Lakshmana's arrows, which are like thunderbolts, run for a short time, and then lie down upon the battlefield. Even the leader of the demons, seeing many of his sons fallen, has left his attack upon Ráma, and fearing evil, rushes swiftly to the side of Meghanáda. Therefore I fear this may prove a misfortune.

INDRA.

King of aerial spirits! What misfortune can happen here? These scions of the race of Kakutstha are invincible in might. For just as the chiefs of the night-stalkers, more than thousands in number, are but one mark to that hero; so is the ten-headed one also, though he is the pride of the assembly of warriors who excel in battle.

CHITRARATHA.

King of gods! when an attack is made by many upon

one, a glorious termination falls not to the lot of many mortals. (*With surprise.*) Let the king of gods look here. When the chief of demons issued forth in haste, Kumbhakarna, though eager for the war, was dismayed, pierced by the arrows of the leader of the Raghus. And Kumbha too, when he saw his father brought to this state, rushed to the attack with speed, like to pride embodied or a lofty and moving mountain. (*With surprise.*) Oh! the ease with which the monkey race can enter an aperture! Since a monkey suddenly opposed midway upon the field of battle Kumbha, who was swiftly rushing to attack the first scion of the race of Daca-ratha. (*Looking very intently.*) What! Sugríva indeed! (*With misgiving.*) He, who cannot brook resistance, has fiercely crushed him in his stalwart arms, and flinging him to the ground, trampled upon him, and pounded him as one pounds grain. (*With fear.*) And Kumbhakarna, when he saw this, rushed to the attack, and running very furiously, seized Sugríva; but he, skilfully releasing himself, cut off Kumbhakarna's nose, and thus at the same time took away the shame of his sister.

INDRA.

King of aerial spirits! Look here! The chief of Raghus has quickly achieved a very wondrous exploit upon Meghanáda the leader of demons, whereby he has suddenly brought blindness upon the enemy. Alas! a requital very difficult to be wrought has here overtaken the descendant of Raghu. For, as soon as he shook off the serpent-like meshes hurled by Meghanáda, which by the power of spells approach unperceived, and are hard to be broken, by employing the weapons of the chief of birds; immediately the leader of the demons wounded him deeply in the heart with his hundred-killing weapon, fiercely, and in great anger, so that he fell suddenly upon Hanúman, swooning and helpless.

CHITRARATHA.

King of gods! here is a very wondrous conflict. For when he learned the fainting of his brother from the future king of Lańká, Ráma, with his inner feelings made known by the sorrowful state of the hero, longed to see him even in that state; and though he was surrounded on all sides disorderly by the army of the demons headed by Kumbhakarna, he then again wrought this remedy; since that mighty chieftain of the Raghus attained in form that very state which aforetime the destroyer of cities assumed in his conquest of Tripura, and after cutting to pieces in a moment the younger brother of the king of demons with his arrows, reduced to ashes also his army, and went eagerly towards his younger brother. (*Watching closely.*) Ah! the passing affection of the chief of the Raghus! whereby he understood the state of his younger brother the moment he perceived him. (*Looking round with joy.*) By good fortune I see there is safety for these princes of the race of Raghu; since in this great ocean of calamity that threatens these two, fear has seized upon the leader of the demons with his followers from the death of Kumbhakarna. (*Again looking at both of them.*) How is it that they are still insensible? This silence that is come upon them is of evil hap, since the demons have many wiles, but the enemy is utterly helpless ; such is their state, while the monkeys their allies are also powerless. I know not therefore what destiny will do in this case.

INDRA.

King of aerial spirits! why hast thou this distrust? See, the son of the wind, the chief of those whose greatness is beyond thought, lives and comes to his senses. He now, with the hair bristling from the pores of his skin, resembling a shower of dust whirling round at the destruction of the world, while the circle of stars is cast aside by the huge sweep of his tail bent a little at the end, with energy corresponding to his zeal has leaped up high in his strength, and after going to some place or other in a moment has wisely returned bringing a huge mountain.

CHITRARATHA (*thoughtfully and pleased*).

King of gods, see! Like a cluster of lotuses by the influence of the moonlight, like iron by the influence of the magnet-stone, like one who has entered the ocean of existence by the influence of true knowledge sweet as nectar, so these two by the breeze from the mountain brought by Hanúman suddenly revive. The power of things is indeed hard to be understood. (*Looking towards the south.*) What! here is the king of Lanká. Again he comes against the enemy bringing with him the army of demons, like the water of the ocean which breaks from its boundary at the end of the age. (*Reflecting.*) But this time the cowardly demons, though many thousands in number consider not about these two, that they despised that army though its chief men were numerous and unshackled by scruples of honourable warfare, and destroyed it so as to leave Rávana and Meghanáda alone remaining. (*Again watching Lakshmana.*) Thus like a jewel cut upon the stone, like the sun free from dense clouds, like a sword drawn from the scabbard, or a hooded serpent casting its skin, suddenly the chief of Raghus shines forth. What can be the cause? What other than the divine healing plant, whose greatness and inconceivable power prevails? (*Watching.*) What! the battle is again commenced by the warriors that march in the van of the monkeys and demons; for on the battlefield one army with sharp arrows, the other with fierce claws, their minds full of self-pride, pierce each other with repeated blows; and they wear on their breast, late scented with fragrant powder, the dust of the ground upraised in the furious conflict. (*Examining closely.*) The difference perceptible between these two armies is like that between deep darkness and the light of dawn in the morning twilight; for this army of demons each moment decreases more and more, while the infinite qualities of the monkeys increase.

INDRA.

King of aerial spirits! a great slaughter has again been begun on this side. The son of Rávana, leader of the demons, and Lakshmana, chief of the Raghus, have suddenly joined in single combat; and, while their skill in the bow is seen in the passing strength of their throbbing arms, since each has an equal power of resistance to the use of charmed weapons, they have made their troops feel contempt for the flames that will spread at the world's end.

CHITRARATHA.

King of gods! This deadly conflict between the two mighty warriors cannot easily be prevented; for they have long filled the heavens with their shouts, the sky with showers of arrows, and the surface of the earth with the bodies of their enemies cleft in two; and they cause us, as we look on, to lose the range of vision, which is dimmed with streams of tears, and to be covered with bristling hair rising up and full of trembling. (*Looking very fixedly.*) How is it that only one thing becomes very conspicuous, ascertained both by perception and inference; since I see that the conduct of Rághava is ten times superior to the conduct of Rávana, and I infer that it is infinitely superior from the death of the demons that fall at his side? (*Looking round with curiosity and surprise.*) All those night-stalkers, as many as went forth from the city, with their banner-like arms waving the sword, fighting front to front with the enemy, and incited by the pride of their throbbing limbs, have been strangely reduced in a moment to the state of locusts in the fire-like splendour of Dácarathi, which is fanned with wind from the wings of showers of hurled arrows. (*Thoughtfully.*) Such indeed is this creation composed of the five elements! Those demons, for whom even the three worlds were not sufficient to stand upon, now in death rest on this lower world only.

INDRA.

King of aerial spirits! See! Those two, Ráma and Rávana, excite wonder by their combat; for Rávana, whose heads are swiftly cut off by the arrows of the two sons of Raghu, being but one seems like many, and those two with their pleasing qualities deserve the praise of the enemy; and as they merely watch for a long time, a glory beyond description attaches to them, while their energy and courage fail not, and their arrows also cease not to cut the hero's heads.

(*A voice is heard behind the scenes.*)

O Rámabhadra! why even now dost thou lightly regard this wicked one? Why neglect this matter which ought to be accomplished at once? Just listen. Your majesty should obtain Sítá; the people who are in the three worlds the joy that is proper; the young descendant of Pulastya the city, and Rávana here his own immortality. What more can be said here? The assembly of saints, to whom the highest truth has been revealed, should receive peace in their minds, in which joy is increased by calmness.

CHITRARATHA (*listening*).

What! here is a company of divine sages urging on the two sons of Raghu to destroy their foes. To whose mind does not the destruction of the wicked give pleasure? (*Hurriedly and with great eagerness.*) King of gods! See! The heads of Rávana, the chief of demons, and of his son after him, were cut off by the two sons of Raghu with arrows, effectual by help of remembering the immortal arms of the supreme; and then on the battlefield the headless trunks of the demons, and with them the demon-women frantic with grief, fell upon the ground; but on the head of the glorious sons of Dacaratha fell a shower of flowers from the sky.

INDRA (*looking towards the tiring-room and with delight*).

King of aerial spirits! See! The gods here filled with joy upon hearing the tidings of the death of the ten-headed one, the enemy of the three worlds, accompanied by sages of placid minds wish to keep some festival, and are waiting only for me. I will therefore go to gratify their wish. Do thou too gladden the ruler of Alaká, our dear friend, by informing him of these tidings.

[*All walk round and then retire.*

END OF THE SIXTH ACT.

ACT VII.

Enter the PATRON GODDESS *of* LANKÁ *full of grief.*

LANKÁ (*with loud lamentations*).

Alas! great King Rávana! thou that wast pampered by thy marriage with the goddess of warriors in the three worlds, thou that didst wrongly pride thyself on thy stalwart arms able to protect the whole world of demons! Alas! thou that didst offer up thy lotus-like centre face when thou didst worship the feet of the lord of creatures! Alas! thou glory of the sons of Kaikasí. Alas! thou that didst tenderly love the circle of thy kinsfolk! where can I see thee? Alas! Prince Kumbhakarna! Alas! dear Meghanáda! where art thou? give me an answer. (*Looking round.*) How is it that no one speaks? (*Looking up.*) Alas! cruel sport of destiny! why art thou thus changed? And yet what blame attaches to destiny for this? Surely it is only his own bad actions that are come to this evil end.

[*Thus with loud lamentations she weeps.*

Enter ALAKÁ.

Alas! since of the company of demons, so great as it was, even in a moment only Vibhíshana is left; how is it that this change of state, strange and unparallelled, has befallen the king of demons? (*Listening to the sound.*) What! here is my young sister Lanká wailing and afflicted with grief at the late bereavement of her husband. (*Approaching.*) Sister, be comforted.

LANKÁ (*reflecting*).

What! my sister Alaká.

ALAKÁ.

Sister, be comforted. Such indeed is the way of the world.

LANKÁ.

Ah, sister! whence can I have comfort? I am bereaved of everything save my maidens, while the Prince Vibhíshana alone remains to continue the race. But even he by reason of our sad misfortune serves the enemy.

ALAKÁ.

Ah, sister! 'tis not so; he is not indeed our enemy.

LANKÁ.

How so?

ALAKÁ.

He to whom he was an enemy is gone, and the enmity is gone. But now the son of Dacaratha, whose prosperity is famous in the three worlds, is our natural friend.

LANKÁ (*reviving*).

What! is he such?

ALAKÁ.

He is indeed.

LANKÁ.

How can he who was such towards our kings have so changed?

ALAKÁ.

Why dost thou thus speak without due inquiry? Listen! When the pride of the race of Raghu attended only by his brother at the command of his father entered the Dandaká forest, proper* treatment was shown him by this thy ruler of the demons, and this is the full result of that action.

LANKÁ.

But why art thou come hither at such a moment as this?

ALAKÁ.

When his half-brother, descendant of Pulastya, learned these tidings from Chitraratha, the king of aerial spirits, he sent me to instruct his kinsmen that are left, and openly to install Vibhíshana in the kingdom of Lanká, and to give directions for presenting Rámabhadra with the chariot, the best of cars, that was carried off by Rávana.

LANKÁ.

Ah! how is it that even the lord of treasures, the friend of the divine ruler of creatures, himself honours Rámabhadra?

ALAKÁ.

What wonder at this? He, indeed, is the truth to those who possess the highest knowledge; he is the ancient male visible before us; he is nature triply divided, of himself come down to protect the good upon earth.

LANKÁ.

But how could our lord the king of demons be ignorant of this?

* This is said in irony, she really means improper treatment.

ALAKÁ.

Ah, my dear sister! Seeing that his infatuation was increased by the greatness of a curse, he is guilty of no trespass.

[*A noise behind the scenes. Both listen eagerly.*

(*Again a cry behind the scenes.*)

Give heed, you creatures that move in the three worlds. The god of great renown (Indra) accompanied by Vasu, Arka, and Rudra, is come in person to salute the virtuous lady. Do thou, best of the Raghus, honour Sítá who is the stay of thy life, and whose purity is declared by her entering and coming out of the fire.

ALAKÁ.

What! even the gods here salute the divine Sítá, who has entered and come forth from the fire, in order to dispel the suspicion of the rumour of unchastity arising from her residence in the house of Rávana. The glory of faithfulness to her husband is increased by another glory. This is a marvel, or perhaps it is in accordance with the way of the world.

LANKÁ (*listening*).

What! Songs blended with auspicious notes are heard.

ALAKÁ (*looking towards the tiring-room*).

Ah! Vibhíshana, whose happy inaguration has been performed at the command of Rámabhadra by nymphs who are come down to congratulate Sítá on her purity, and by divine sages, comes towards Rámabhadra in a celestial car. Come then, let us satisfy our eyes by beholding the high-minded one who is deserving of praise for his peerless and natural greatness.

[*They walk round and leave the stage.*

END OF THE VISHKAMBHAKA.

Enter VIBHÍSHANA *in a celestial car.*

I have carried out the command of Rámabhadra; for honour was paid to Mátali, and after him the captive women who belong to the world of gods, whose cheeks were marked with wounds made by floods of tears that fall without ceasing, while their golden bracelets dropped down, wearing only one braid of smooth hair, with garments very miry from rolling upon the ground, went forth with smiles. (*Approaching.*) Success to Rámabhadra. Sire, your command, which thus concluded, is accomplished. The prison-houses, that were filled with captive women, are now adorned with chains of gold worthy to be seen, and with banners. And here is that best of chariots, called Pushpaka, unimpeded in its motion, of coveted speed, under control, the action of which is ever obedient to the will.

RÁMA.

'Tis well, O king of Lanká! 'tis well done. (*Towards Sugríva.*) Friend, descendant of the sun, what now remains?

SUGRÍVA.

That bane of the three worlds, although his greatness was declared by his haughty stalwart arms, has been rooted out; and the outrage to the divine Sítá has been atoned for; and a treaty has here been concluded by inaugurating the all-excellent Vibhíshana. But now the Prince Bharata, who heard the news with all its details from Hanúman, who was bringing the mountain Drona, is sorely afflicted. Let the son of the wind be dispatched to bear tidings to him, and do thou adorn the best of chariots.

RÁMA.

At the pleasure of our dear friend.

[*He mounts the car.*

(*All gesticulate an ascent of the chariot.*)

SÍTÁ (*speaking aside to Lakshmana*).

Where shall we go now?

LAKSHMANA.

O queen! to Ayodhyá, the capital of the race of the Raghus.

SÍTÁ.

Is the period of our residence in the forest ended?

LAKSHMANA.

It is, O queen! this very day.

[*All watch the motion of the chariot.*

SÍTÁ (*with surprise*).

Prince! what are these neighbouring places that are

seen in the distance, the southern part of which we cannot determine, and the darkness of which extends on all sides?

RÁMA.

These, O queen! are the confines of the earth; but visible there is the first form of the eight-formed one, consisting of water, and called by men ocean, the inner depth of which is beyond limit.

SÍTÁ.

The form of which was made by our ancient fathers-in-law, thus it is said in the tradition of the learned. But what is this that appears in the middle of it, like a white garment spread widely in the parts that are covered with fresh grass?

LAKSHMANA.

O queen! this is the new causeway seen in the ocean like a pillar of fame to tell the exploits of the noble one, built by the leaders of the monkeys who carried out the command of their chief with energy and pleasure, and who caused the peaks of tall mountains to be brought from the ends of the quarters, the greatness of which is worthy of worship to the world's end.

RÁMA (*pointing with his finger*).

O brother! thou rememberest these parts, where circles of creeper-houses covered with dew are darkened by the shade of clustering Tamála-trees, and where full and clear streams of cataracts fall from the top of the high peak of the Malaya mountain?

LAKSHMANA.

Brother! they are those parts indeed; and not far hence is that old cavern where we passed the night, while the heavens were rent with roars, and the huge cloud, deafening with peals of thunder, kept rolling in the sky through the fury of the storm-wind, and the deep darkness of the trees as it met the eye confused and blinded it, and the rain-cloud poured. I know it by the bamboos.

SÍTÁ (*speaking to herself*).

Alas! the thoughtlessness! Why did I, unhappy one that I am, cause these high-minded heroes to experience so different a state at the hands of the demons?

VIBHÍSHANA.

King Rámabhadra! here the lands on the bank of the river Kaverí are seen, and on the skirts of the neighbouring mountain the numerous hermitages are known by the tall and decayed trees, by the grounds covered with betel-trees, close, pouring showers of sap from the Kuhalî trees; where dwell saints to whom the supreme has been revealed in their firm penance and meditation, and who are witnesses to the duration of the world. And not far hence towards the south, in the ground adorned by Lopamudrá, there shines a splendour arising from the saint Agastya.

RÁMA.

What! Is the hermitage of Agastya passed? He, in whose sport this ocean became a desert, and by whom the Vindhya mountain was spoiled of its play and gave up its increase; and in the fire of whose belly the body of the demon Vátápi melted. Within the range of whose speech does that saint of unimpaired soul come? Hence those high-minded ones are powerful beyond measure, and witnesses of the inner soul of the universe. How then are they not worthy to be bowed down to?

[*All bow.*

(*A voice is heard in the sky.*)

Do thou, with thy younger brother, protect the people. May thy fame abide to the end of the world! May thy name "Ráma" be able to give immortality to those who pronounce it!

RÁMA (*listening*).

What! He who makes obeisance to the great sage is highly favoured with a voice that possesses not a body.

[*The rest applaud.*

VIBHÍSHANA.

King Rámabhadra! These are the places in the neighbourhood of the river Pampá, where the tokens perceived after a long time forcibly attract the eye; for a part of that decayed palm-tree which was pierced by a single arrow shines in front; and here by reason of countless shafts the famed Válí experienced only for a moment the monkey-state he assumed in play. Saumitri here cast aside easily with a kick of his foot the heap of bones. Your majesty saw the state of the headless demon, and the upper garment of the queen in the hand of Hanúman.

SÍTÁ (*to herself*).

Was my upper garment seen by the prince in the hand of Hanúman?

RÁMA (*remembering*).

Ah, queen! when you were carried away helplessly, your upper garment fell, and that was the first token we obtained. As soon as it was seen, it became like the brightness of an autumn moon to our eyes, and a shower of camphor-powder to the body, and copious sprinkling from a jar of nectar to the mind.

[SÍTÁ *gesticulates shame*.

LAKSHMANA.

That vulture king, the friend of our father, quickly following the wicked demon in this forest, left his limbs enfeebled by old age, and obtained a new body of renown.

SÍTÁ (*to herself*).

How is it that such deep distress is said to have befallen those high-minded heroes on account of me?

SUGRÍVA.

Queen! We are passing over those boundaries of the Dandaká forest where the demons Trimúrddhan, Khara, and Dúshana with their followers went somewhere in their desire to search for the lips, nose, and ears of their sister.

SÍTÁ (*trembling*).

Alas! how is it that the demons are again heard?

RÁMA.

O queen, away with thy fear. Their name alone is left. The destruction of the demons arises from the mere twang of the bow of Saumitri, as the destruction of elephants from the roar of the lion. (*Looking intently*). What! the motion of this most excellent of chariots seems changed.

VIBHÍSHANA.

O sire! This mountain Sahya is very high indeed, and must be passed in order to reach Áryyavartta. Therefore, in order to surmount it, even this chariot leaves a little its proximity to the middle world.

LAKSHMANA.

The middle world, marked by the feet of the first male, is worthy to be seen.

[*All watch closely the speed of their ascent.*

RÁMA (*beholding with astonishment*).

The visible god, author of the ancestors of our race, treasure of splendours, great essence of the three Vedas endowed with a form, the sun, is very near through the ascent of the heavenly chariot.

[*All bow, folding their hands into the form of a dove.*

SÍTÁ (*looking up*).

Ah! how is it that even in the daytime there appears as it were this circle of stars?

RÁMA.

Queen! it is indeed a circle of stars; but owing to

the great distance we cannot perceive it in the daytime; as our eyes are dimmed by the rays of the sun. Now, that distance is removed by the ascent of the chariot.

SÍTÁ (*with surprise*).

How comes it that flowers seem to be blooming in the garden of the sky?

RÁMA (*looking round*).

Ah! the world seems to have the divisions of its quarters indefinable, for the traces of the earth cannot be clearly perceived by reason of the distance, but those of the sky seem everywhere the same.

SUGRÍVA.

O king! I well remember what time I was united in friendship to my brother, and wandered at will in the ends of the world; for these are the two mountains where the sun rises and sets, in the lap of which the sun and moon pass infancy and old age in ease and without fear. Look here, O king! these are the two mountains Kailása and Áñjana, equal in height and width, like the two breasts of the earth tinted with sandal and musk. And here is the golden mountain, and next is the mountain Gandhamádana, the peaks of which touch the sky; and after that are the lands impassable to such as me.

RÁMA (*looking round and speaking hurriedly and with surprise*).

How is it that everything suddenly comes within the

range of the eye? And the order of creation is clearly determined.

SÍTÁ.

Oh! some object here appears, unseen before, and strange indeed. It is neither man nor beast.

RÁMA.

Queen! This is a pair of horse-headed demigods. Such spirits as these roam in great numbers in these districts.

VIBHÍṢHANA.

What! They are coming towards us, perhaps they may bring some command from the king of Alaká.

(*A voice behind the scenes.*)

O king, jewel in the race of the sun! Rámabhadra! as we were going to Sáketa to praise your majesty commanded by the king of the mountain of demigods, thou didst appear before our sight midway, because of the propriety of our journey. Obedience to his command tends to great merit, for thus is perceived that splendour which belongs to the order of manifestations of the ancient male.

[*They pass round to the right and praise him. All look on.*

(A DEMIGOD *behind the scenes.*)

O Rámabhadra! thou who art kind to the distressed and the sole friend to the people in the world! thou who art to the wise as a cluster of lotuses to swans! May thy fame for a thousand years be enjoyed by the good, who are like to chakora birds, and who are perplexed by birth, and the like events of life.

(A FEMALE SPIRIT *behind the scenes.*)

As long as this orb of the world endures on the head of the chief of serpents ;—as long as the sky is decked with hosts of stars ; so long, O Vaidehi ! may thy praise, spotless and holy, be sung in the world by those of noble conduct.

THE REST.

We are well pleased.

RÁMA.

O king of Lańká ! from long walking I find no pleasure in this place, it is better therefore that we should go hence, nearer the middle world.

VIBHÍSHANA.

These are the pure feet of the father of Gaurí, whose rocks are washed by the river of the gods, and shine with portions of camphor, and have the bark of decayed birch trees ; where there ever shines a lustre—naturally pleasant and bright—of the saints, the darkness of whose ignorance has been dispelled by the light of truth, and who possess a knowledge of the supreme spirit, and know the Veda.

LAKSHMANA.

Noble brother ! how is it that these neighbouring places of the earth suffer not our eye to perceive any other objects that were before well known ?

RÁMA (*looking and remembering quickly*).

Brother! here are the grounds of the penance grove of the saints, the neighbourhood of which is made pure by the walking of Kaucika's feet; where the second king of Videha, the honoured pupil of Yájńavalkya, and the saints who enjoyed the nectar-like pleasure of his conversation, sported with us, and we indulged in the play that is proper for infancy.

SÍTÁ (*to herself*).

What! do I hear the name of my uncle?

[*She looks eagerly round.*

RÁMA.

O king of Lanká! it is not proper now to ride in the chariot in these districts that are purified by the lotus-like feet of our preceptor.

(*A voice behind the scenes.*)

O Ráma and Lakshmana! the holy pupil of Kricácva commands you.

BOTH (*making a sign to the goddess of the chariot to stop it*).

We are attentive.

(*Again a voice behind the scenes.*)

Do you two go to the city as you are, and delay not on the way; the glory that accompanies Arundhatí awaits you there. I also, who am busy now performing the rites of the third season, will come in two hours.

BOTH.

As our instructors command.

[*Again they urge on the chariot.*

RÁMA.

Oh! even these high-minded ones are full of compassion, so great that, although the time of their penance and meditation is divided into small portions, even in that small portion they watch for our approach. Perhaps it is seemly, since by the fulness of their mercy they are kindly disposed towards the deer of the hermitage and the trees. What then are they towards men? Moreover, our birth only is in the house of kings born in the line of the sun; but our training, which consists chiefly in the knowledge of arms and charmed weapons, came from this high-minded priest.

VIBHÍSHANA (*looking*).

How is it that suddenly the skies are covered with the dust of the earth as by showers of dew?

[*All look with surprise.*

RÁMA (*thoughtfully*).

I think Bharata has learned tidings of us from the son of the wind, and is coming with the army to meet me.

Enter HANÚMAN (*bowing so as to touch his feet*).

O sire! Bharata, who stood for a long time thinking of some great deed in his mind, when he learned from me the tidings, started out; and now wearing matted hair and bark dress, and pronouncing the name of Ráma of eternal power, approaches with his whole nature again and again frantic with joy.

RÁMA (*joyfully*).

We are quite overjoyed at the thought that we shall obtain after so long a time the friendship of the prince.

LAKSHMANA (*inquiringly.*)

Friend Hanúman! where is he?

HANÚMAN.

Thou seest those five or six in front of the army. In their midst is the general, the high-minded Bharata, accompanied by his younger brother.

[*Lakshmana looks.*

SÍTÁ (*beholding.*)

What! He appears altered.

VIBHÍSHANA.

O prince of chariots! This moment stop. Let these high-souled ones enjoy the pleasure of each other's embrace, by seeing and clasping in their arms and honouring their kinsfolk after their long separation.

[*All gesticulate a descent from the chariot.*

Enter BHARATA *and* CATRUGHNA *surrounded by several chieftains.*

RÁMA (*quickly raising up Bharata, who had fallen at his feet*).

Come here, brother! This day thy touch, rough as the budding fibre of the best of lotuses, makes me almost realise the pleasure of the supreme.

[*After closely embracing he lets him go.*

(LAKSHMANA *falls at the feet of* BHARATA *and embraces him.* CATRUGHNA *salutes* RÁMA *and* LAKSHMANA.)

RÁMA AND LAKSHMANA.

Honour the stay of our race!

(BHARATA *and* CATRUGHNA *bow down prostrate before* SÍTÁ.)

SÍTÁ.

O Princes! may you be welcome to your elder brothers.

RÁMA.

Dear Bharata and Catrughna! This king of monkeys here became a boat to us in the ocean of our calamity; and here is his friend, the king of Lanká, ever engaged in the cause of holiness. Therefore embrace them.

[*He points to Sugríva and Vibhíshana.*

(BHARATA *and* CATRUGHNA *embrace them and pay the customary honours.*)

BHARATA.

Noble brother! Our family preceptor the holy Maitrávaruni, has collected together all the vessels for inauguration that you may ascend the throne, and awaits your majesty's command.

RÁMA (*speaking to himself*).

The feet of Kaucika are worthy of respect, and the holy Maitrávaruni makes this request. Be it so, a suitable answer shall be given. (*Aloud.*) As our family preceptor requests.

[*All walk round.*

Enter VASISHTHA *and* ARUNDHATÍ *attended by the wives of Dacaratha.*

VASISHTHA (*to himself*).

We are very busy about Ráma from the joy we feel at the thought that he is worshipped here externally by the eye—he who is the support of the earth, and full of virtues like a mine of countless precious stones, the embodied development of the good deeds of those mortals whom he has succoured, and pleasant by reason of his mercy. Be it so, still we must follow the way of the world. (*Aloud.*) You wives Kaucalyá and Sumitrá!

BOTH.

Let the family preceptor command us.

VASISHTHA.

Your children are returned to you unscathed.

BOTH.

'Tis due to the power of your blessings.

ARUNDHATÍ (*looking at Kaikeyí*).

Daughter Kaikeyí! why art thou thus afflicted?

KAIKEYÍ.

Mother! Through my misfortune, wretched woman that I am, even the whole world speaks vile words, saying that through the mouth of Manthará the second mother became the cause of her children's exile. How, therefore, can I behold their face?

ARUNDHATÍ.

Daughter! Away with thy false fears of slander. The noble princes at once perceived this matter with their inner eye.

ALL.

How so?

ARUNDHATÍ.

Cúrpanakhá wearing the form of Manthará did this at the instigation of Málayaván.

ALL.

Alas! the wicked plots of the demons that pain even the women that stand here!

VASISHTHA.

On this happy occasion, away with all sorrow. Why even on this day is there mention of the plots of demons?

RÁMA (*beholding Vasishtha joyfully*).

Here is the holy Maitrávaruni, at the sight of whom my mind seems to melt, as the moon-stone melts in the light of the full moon. (*Speaking to Lakshmana.*) Brother, come here.

BOTH (*approaching*).

Honoured preceptor of our race! Ráma and Lakshmana salute you.

VASISHTHA.

Do you two, my children, whenever you have leisure, be to my eyes an ornament preceded by modesty, holiness, and knowledge.

(*Both salute* ARUNDHATÍ.)

ARUNDHATÍ.

May your desires be gratified.

(*Both salute all the Mothers in order.*)

ALL OF THEM (*embracing* RÁMA *and* LAKSHMANA *and kissing their head*).

May that which we are thinking of befall you.

(SÍTÁ *approaches and salutes* VASISHTHA.)

VASISHTHA.

Daughter! Mayst thou become the mother of a hero.

(SÍTÁ *salutes* ARUNDHATÍ.)

ARUNDHATÍ (*closely embracing* SÍTÁ).

Lopámudrá, Anasúyá, myself and thou,—let the chaste wives be now, O Jánakí! four in number.

(SÍTÁ *salutes her Mothers-in-law.*)

ALL.

Daughter! Mayest thou become the mother of a prince who will prove the support of the race.

(*A voice behind the scenes.*)

Citizens! go to your homes, and celebrate the festival to-day. And you, officers, attend long to your respective duties. And you, Bráhmans! place here the vessels as ordered; the chief of the Kucikas, the pupil of Kricácva, commands you.

VASISHTHA (*listening*).

Oh! this is due to the excellent good fortune of the prince, that the divine Kaucika is come in person to place him on the throne.

THE REST.

We are pleased.

Enter VICVÁMITRA *attended by pupils.*

VICVÁMITRA.

The plan that I formed in my mind when I took him from the hand of Dacaratha to destroy the enemies of sacrifice, and the energy that was shown in the corresponding act have, through the propitiousness of destiny and the might of his efforts, borne fruits to us, and we are now satisfied after anointing the glorious Ráma in the kingdom; and at the thought of this we are more and more pleased. [*He walks round.*

VASISHTHA.

This is that Kaucika, whose natural glory as a warrior and whose splendour as a Bráhman exceed all. What is there in him, a store of wonder surpassing the world, that is not astonishing?

(VASISHTHA *and* VICVÁMITRA *approach and salute each other.*)

VICVÁMITRA.

Honoured Maitrávaruni! what dost thou wish to-day.

VASISHTHA.

Let the proper sacrifice be made.

VICVÁMITRA (*addressing the assembly of divine sages*).

Let the inauguration of Rámabhadra be made.

[*The rest carry out what is necessary.*

(*A sound of celestial drums behind the scenes. All behold with wonder a shower of flowers.*)

VASISHTHA.

What! The divine Indra with the world's guardians approves of the inauguration of Rámabhadra.

RÁMA (*who has received the auspicious rites of inauguration, approaching* VASISHTHA *and* VIÇVÁMITRA).

O preceptors! I salute you.

BOTH.

O Rámabhadra, pleasing by thy virtues! Do thou, attended by thy brother, bear the burden that has long been borne by the kings of earth, headed by Ikshváku.

THE REST.

Let it be so.

VIÇVÁMITRA.

Son Rámabhadra!

RÁMA.

Let my teachers give me their commands.

VIÇVÁMITRA.

Let Sugríva and Vibhíshana, who have felt the joy of the festival, be dismissed; and let the car, which can easily be had whenever it is desired, go to the king of kings. [RÁMA *does so.*

VIÇVÁMITRA.

Son Rámabhadra! The harsh command of thy father was borne, and his duty was performed, and the three worlds had their mental sickness cured by the destruction of the demons; the gods were satisfied, and the kingdom was won by thee, accompanied by thy younger brother, friends, and wife. What more than this can be done? Let that favour too be declared.

RÁMA.

Can any favour be greater than this? However, be this also with the approval of your majesty. May the guardians of the world, free from indolence, protect the orb of the earth. May the clouds pour down their rain in due season; may the whole kingdom be free from calamity, and supplied with grain: may poets make sweet verses, which will give undying pleasure to the world; and may the learned go forth and teach men to delight in the compositions of others.

VICVÁMITRA.

May it be so. [*Exeunt omnes.*

THE END.